ROYAL ADMIRALS
1327–1981

By the same author

WITH ENSIGNS FLYING
The Story of British Destroyers in World War II

SUBMARINE VICTORY
The Story of British Submarines in World War II

BATTLE OF THE JAVA SEA

CRETE 1941 : THE BATTLE AT SEA
(Published in the USA as NAZI VICTORY)

JAPAN'S WAR AT SEA
Pearl Harbor to the Coral Sea

Royal Admirals
1327–1981

David A. Thomas

ANDRE DEUTSCH

ACKNOWLEDGEMENTS

The author and publisher would like to thank the following for permission to reproduce photographs from their collections:

Her Majesty the Queen; Broadlands Archives; British Library; British Museum; Crown Copyright; Daily Express Newspapers; Guildhall Library; Illustrated London Newspapers; Imperial War Museum; Leicester Art Gallery; National Maritime Museum, Greenwich; National Portrait Gallery; Rijksmuseum, Amsterdam; St Bartholomew's Hospital; Tate Gallery; Victoria and Albert Museum; Woodmansterne.

First published 1982 by
André Deutsch Limited
105 Great Russell Street London WC1

Printed in Great Britain by
Ebenezer Baylis and Son Ltd, Worcester

British Library Cataloguing in
Publication Data
Thomas, David
   Royal admirals 1327–1981.
   1. Naval history, Modern
   2. Great Britain—Kings and rulers—
   History
   I. Title
   359.4'09   D436

ISBN 0-233-97427-X

Contents

1

Founders of a Heritage

KING ALFRED is recorded as having gone to sea in 882 in his early thirties and having destroyed four Danish ships. Three years later he sent a force of ships from the Medway across the Thames estuary to East Anglian waters. In the Stour estuary, opposite where Harwich now stands 'they met sixteen ships of pirates and fought against them and captured all the ships and slew the crews. When they were on their way home with the booty they met a great fleet of pirates and fought against them the same day, and the Danes were victorious.' This engagement, a far cry from the Battles of Lowestoft, Solebay and Jutland, nevertheless might justly be called the first action of British naval history.

Alfred, called The Great, King of the West Saxons in the ninth century AD, was a Titan. He was a leader of vision, a mighty soldier, a splendid administrator, a lawgiver and protector: a man for all seasons. Rarely in history is the appellation The Great accorded to anyone. Alfred earned it by his deeds. Not for centuries was an English monarch to do battle with the resounding success that crowned Alfred's lifelong years of struggle and fierce ordeals against the Danes. With Churchillian defiance he roused his people and achieved triumph and victory from defeat and disaster.

An intellectual, a scholar and author, a pious Christian and founder of monasteries, he had the broader vision in war to engage the invaders before they entered the estuaries and set foot on English soil.

It was in 896—Alfred's Silver Jubilee year—that he ordered more ships to be built to meet the continuing threat of the Danish longships on their pillaging visits. His father and brother before him had built a navy of sorts but it was Alfred who not only first

I

King Alfred is shown here inciting the Saxons to prevent the landing of the Danes. The painting, by G. F. Watts, hangs in the House of Lords. (Crown Copyright)

appreciated the need of the Saxons to build numerous ships but also to train men to be at least as competent as the Danes in handling them. He also propounded the strategy of intercepting the pirates at sea when in relatively defenceless positions, crowded in their long, narrow vessels, vulnerable to ramming, with crews that could be shot at with arrows as they manned the oars.

Alfred himself favoured oared ships rather than purely sailing vessels. Perhaps he had been influenced by ships of the Mediterranean which he would have seen during childhood visits to Rome.* There, oared galleys with beaked prows for ramming the enemy outclassed ships of sail. *The Anglo-Saxon Chronicle* tells us that Alfred's ships 'were twice as long as the others, some had sixty oars, some more; they were faster and steadier and had more freeboard. They were not built after the Danish or Friesian design, but in the way the king thought would be most effective.' For these modest

* As a twelve-year-old boy on the first of two pilgrimages to Rome, in 853 and 855, he met the Pope, Leo IV.

achievements historians wrongly dubbed him 'Father of the Navy'. But there was some justification for the nickname, and his reign serves as a reasonable base on which to build the story of Britain's heritage of royal service at sea.

It was three-quarters of a century later that Alfred's great-grandson, King Edgar, who reigned from 959–975, is reported to have received the homage of eight British inferior or sub-kings at his delayed coronation performed, curiously, fourteen years after his succession to the throne. Edgar had travelled north by sea to Chester. There, six of the sub-kings rowed him as a symbol of homage and submission on the River Dee while Edgar held the steering oar, attended by a concourse of nobles, enjoying the height of majesty.

Edgar, like Alfred, owned few ships of war. The later Norman chronicle of Edgar's adventures referred to his 3600 ships, divided into three parts—east, west and north—but this referred to the number of ships owned by loyal subjects which could be hired or mobilized by the King in times of emergency. It is reported, too, that Edgar undertook cruises each year of his reign to inspect this substantial fleet of ships, each cruise lasting all summer long.

It was King Edward the Confessor (1004–1066), founder of Westminster Abbey, who rationalized this rather makeshift arrangement of having a motley collection of ships at one's command by founding the Confederation of the Cinque Ports, an ancient maritime institution lasting—in name at least—to this day.

Hastings, Romney, Hythe, Dover and Sandwich were the original ports to which were added later Winchelsea and Rye. They had jurisdiction along the south coast from Seaford in Sussex to Birchington in Kent and they undertook to furnish the King with a fleet of ships for a specified period each year. In return the port barons were given tax exemptions and many legal privileges including a right, within wide limits, to make their own laws in their own parliaments and to administer them in their own courts. For some centuries these towns played a central part in English maritime history until the fifteenth century, chiefly in providing armed transports for English armies to cross the Channel. But by Tudor times all these ports except Dover had begun to show signs of silting and their rights and obligations had fallen into decline and all that remains today, nine hundred years later, is the ceremonial sinecure of the office of the Lord Wardenship of the Cinque Ports. The current Lord Warden whose induction, accompanied by splendid pageantry, took place in 1979, is Her Majesty Queen Elizabeth the Queen Mother. The Cinque Ports emblem, half lion and half ship, is depicted upon the Cinque Ports flag which has been flown proudly by earlier Wardens, including among their number Sir Winston Churchill, William Pitt the Younger and the Iron Duke.

None of the medieval kings we have mentioned—Alfred, Edgar, Edward the Confessor—can be said to have been royal admirals in the sense that they were not true sailors, but each contributed significantly to the naval heritage of this island race, albeit in a defensive role, for all three regarded the sea not as a defensive moat but as a threat providing an open door to any aggressor. It was a later Edward, embarking from a Cinque Port, who was to display a seamanlike aggression in leading an English fleet into battle who could most justifiably claim to be called the first Sailor King of England.

But before we stride forward a few centuries to consider his activities we must dwell for a moment on Richard I and King John, both of whom were to exercise a deep influence upon the formation of a Royal Navy.

It was Richard I who set out some basic disciplines in 1190 for the proper maintenance of order in the fleet: 'Anyone who slays a man on board ship shall be thrown into the sea lashed to the corpse; if on land he shall be buried in the ground tied to the corpse. Anyone convicted by lawful witnesses of striking another so as to draw blood shall lose his hand . . . .'

As well as being a disciplinarian Richard was nothing if not a showman: David Beatty and Andrew Cunningham in the two world wars of the twentieth century also knew the value of showmanship as admirals. Crusading on passage to the Holy Land Richard landed on the island of Sicily before making a ceremonial entry into the port of Messina with all pomp and majesty. An eyewitness of the event has left this valuable report:

The populace rushed out eagerly to behold him, crowding along the shore. And lo! on the horizon they saw a fleet of innumerable galleys, and then far off, they could hear the shrill sound of trumpets. As the galleys came nearer they could see that they were painted in different colours and hung with shields glittering in the sun: they could make out standards and pennons fixed to spearheads and fluttering in the breeze. Around the ships the sea boiled as the oarsmen drove them onwards. Then, with trumpet peals ringing in their ears, the onlookers beheld what they had been waiting for: the King of England, magnificently dressed and standing on the raised platform, so that he could see and be seen.

Credit goes to Richard for first perceiving the value of maritime operations in support of land forces during the Crusade. And closer to home, credit is also due to him for laying the foundations of what was to become the important port and dockyard of Ports-

This illustration from the fourteenth-century Chronicle of Kings *shows both King Richard I (top right) and the much maligned King John (bottom left). (The British Library)*

mouth. But he had no naval policy. It was the much maligned King John—of Magna Carta fame—who deserves to be honoured for his patronage of the navy, far more than he has been. Although he never served at sea he took a profound interest in the service. In 1202 he prevailed upon the barons of the Cinque Ports:

> We therefore command and enjoin you by the bounden fealty to us, that as you love us and we trust in you, and as you have sworn to do us good service, you so guard the sea, that no provisions may reach him [King Philip VI of France] there by sea . . .

By 1204 John had forty-five galleys available around the coast from King's Lynn to Gloucester and in the following year ships

5

were being built and fitted out specifically for the king's use. The Royal Navy was being born.

In 1206 John was again commandeering ships:

We command you . . . to hasten immediately on receipt of these letters without let or delay to the ports of Southampton, Kilhaven, Christchurch and Yarmouth, and the other ports in your bailiwicks and detain for service all vessels fit for passage that are able to carry eight or more horses. Man them with able seamen at our cost and send them to Portsmouth so that without hindrance they be there on the eve of Pentecost or if possible earlier. And be careful that each ship be provided with ladders and hurdles . . . And let this matter be executed with such diligence that we may not be losers by your default . . . And write to us at London on the Sunday next after the Ascension of our Lord concerning the steps you have taken in this business . . .

Between 1209 and 1212 more than fifty new ships were launched for the King's navy, a new mole was constructed at Portsmouth and warehouses were erected for stocking ship's tackle and stores. Oars had been ordered by the thousand. Cloth for sails by the thousand ells. It was a time of excitement in the founding of the service. Indeed, if a date needed to be fixed to say when Britannia first began to rule the waves then 1212 would fit the bill. John's fleet was then in command of the Channel; well-laden merchantmen were regularly being taken by English warships as prizes and in the following year the navy was called upon for the first time to save England from invasion. It sought out the French fleet and so savaged it that King Philip abandoned his invasion plan. King John, for all his frailties, deserves greater recognition for his services to the Royal Navy than our maritime nation has given him.

It was to be more than a century before another monarch bestowed upon the navy the interest that Alfred and King John had shown, and this time the King was to lead his fleet into battle in person. Edward III was the King and Sluys was the battle.

Edward III of Windsor, like his predecessor Alfred, was a

colossus among sovereigns. His long reign of fifty years sprawled across the fourteenth century from 1327 to 1377. Before the age of fifteen he had inherited a dishonoured crown from his pathetic father, Edward II, who had been deposed for incompetence, for destroying the Church and for losing Scotland, Ireland and Gascony. The young Edward was burdened by a mother, Isabella, who lived in open adultery with Roger Mortimer. To the north, the kingdom lay open to depredations by bands of Scots since the humiliating defeat of Edward II at Bannockburn in 1314.

But the teenage Edward III quickly grew in stature and wisdom. He soon established his independence, regained the confidence of the nobility and reversed the Bannockburn result in a victory against the Scots at Halidon Hill near Berwick. Abroad, he fought and won brilliant military victories, subduing the French and earning the respect of Europe.

More enduring triumphs were achieved in the arts with his patronage of musicians and writers like the young Geoffrey Chaucer and William of Wykeham, founder of Winchester School and New College, Oxford. He founded the ancient order of the Garter in honour of the beautiful Joan, Countess of Salisbury. Not least among his achievements was his fathering of two famous sons, the Black Prince who, legend has it, appropriated the dead King of Bohemia's motto *Ich Dien* on the battlefield at Crecy, and John of Gaunt, Duke of Lancaster, who himself fathered King Henry IV.

Edward III had one other accomplishment which earned him an appropriate title. He participated in the greatest naval engagement of the Middle Ages and became known as 'King of the Seas'.

The Battle of Sluys was fought in 1340 between a fleet commanded by Edward on the one side and a huge armada of French and Genoese ships assembled off Flanders on the other. The battle had been a long time coming.

By 1336 England and France were drifting into the Hundred Years War with an opening move by the French sending their fleet from Marseilles to the English Channel. In 1338 the French raided Portsmouth and Southampton, where they captured the *Christopher*, and in the following year Dover and Folkestone. A naval force even entered the Thames, prompting the English to plant underwater stakes as a barricade in the river approaches to London.

In its debates Parliament had stressed 'Now the sea should be guarded against enemies so that they . . . should not enter the kingdom to destroy it.'

In February 1340 Edward had returned to London from France heavily in debt to Flemish creditors, leaving his wife Philippa and two babies, perhaps as hostages, pledging his royal crown to return with monies raised in Parliament. While Edward repaired to London, Philip VI of France sent his Fleet of French and Genoese ships up the Channel to Sluys, which was then an important port of northern Europe. Here, the mouth of the Scheldt widened out into a huge estuary with protecting isles forming a vast natural harbour. Today the scene has changed. The estuary has long since silted up and Sluys now lies many miles inland.

Edward prepared to meet the challenge. One has to admire his courage. He was no sailor—he is known to have suffered from seasickness—and he was totally inexperienced as a naval commander, yet he embarked upon what can be described as a major fleet operation.

At the end of May he rode to Ipswich, to the River Orwell, where a few of his ships lay. He was a commanding figure: only twenty-eight years old, well built, long flowing golden hair, and a full set of moustache and beard: he was kingly, expansive, vain, and enjoyed the royal pursuits of battle, hunts and tournaments. He understood weaponry and knew that he stood possessed of a commanding weapon, the qualities of which were unsuspected on the Continent: the longbow. The power of this bow and the skill of the bowmen, acquired in the mountains of Wales and Scotland, had developed to a point where even the finest chain mail was no certain protection.

On arrival in the Orwell, Edward commandeered and summoned merchant shipping from nearby ports in the east and south of England, ordering them to assemble crews with archers, arms and provisions. The response was amazing. Within a fortnight one hundred and forty ships had assembled, mostly single-decked one-masted vessels, but many by this time had had castles or platforms built in them as vantage points for the benefit of the archers. Even so, many people regarded Edward's venture to join battle with the superior enemy fleet by ramming and boarding—the only known method of fighting at sea at that time—akin to insanity.

The Battle of Sluys was fought between ships like this, manned by longbowmen in the forecastle and aftercastle while lancers and swordsmen were crammed on to the maindeck. This illustration is from the fourteenth-century Lutterell Psalter. *(The British Library)*

Edward later wrote to his ten-year-old son, Edward, the future Black Prince, giving details of the battle preparations: 'On Friday about noon we reached the coast of Flanders off Blankenberghe where we sighted our enemy's fleet all packed together in the harbour of Sluys, and because we had missed the tide we anchored for the night.'

The Norman fleet that lay before them was like a forest of masts. It numbered upwards of 200 vessels manned by about 40,000 men. Edward declared—'Please God and Saint George'—his longing to fight the enemy and gain revenge for the Southampton humiliation. In his letter to the young Prince Regent he continued: 'On Saturday, St John's Day, soon after the hour of noon at high tide we

9

entered the port upon our enemies who had assembled their ships in very strong array.' The English fleet had been drawn up in three columns, Edward's cog leading the centre column with ships manned 'so that there was one shipload of men-at-arms between every two of archers'.

The French ships were chained together defensively in four lines, towering, seemingly impregnable like a wall, their decks massed with lancers, slingers and crossbowmen. Among the first rank was the captured *Christopher* together with other captured English ships—*Katherine*, *Edward* and *Rose*.

Two chroniclers tell us precisely what happened: one of them refers to the English ships as 'wooden horses' bringing landsmen into close combat at sea; the naval battle was to be fought on military tactics, a feature of which was the employment of longbowmen. The six-foot longbow of yew had a range of no less than 300 yards and in skilled hands could fire ten or twelve three-foot arrows a minute compared with the crossbow's two. At 200 yards' range it was not supposed to miss its target: hundreds of archers could produce a fearful hail of arrows accompanied by an equally fearful swishing sound which produced effects the like of which were not to be exceeded by infantry missiles until the rifles of the American Civil War five centuries later.

This fourteenth-century illustration shows longbowmen such as those who fought at Sluys. The unpulled bows are shown to be the height of a man. (The British Library)

Edward had mustered about 20,000 men aboard his ships, most of them longbowmen and men-at-arms with their lances and swords. He embarked aboard his cog, the *Thomas*, commanded by Captain Richard Fyall, on Thursday 22 June and sailed throughout that day and night. He was accompanied by five earls—Derby, Pembroke, Hereford, Huntingdon and Gloucester—and numerous knights and lords. Incredibly, according to the great late fourteenth-century historian Sir John Froissart, 'There were on board a large number of noble ladies on their way to Ghent to attend the Queen . . . They were well escorted by 300 men-at-arms and five hundred archers, provided by the king, who besought them to defend his honour.'

Edward advanced his fleet to the sound of trumpets with the wind on the starboard quarter while the sun shone in the eyes of the Frenchmen and the hired Genoese mercenaries whose commanders kept their ships unchained, sensibly preferring the freedom of movement.

As the range closed a fierce battle developed. The hail of English arrows wrought havoc among the enemy crossbowmen and long before the ships collided and grappling irons had been secured, the enemy force was engulfed in defeat. Savage life-or-death hand-to-hand fighting ensued.

The death and destruction among the French was enormous. The *Christopher* was captured early in the engagement and she became a valuable platform for the English archers in attacking the Genoese ships. 'The very air was darkened with arrows . . . the men-at-arms engaged in close fighting.'

By dusk it was all over. Edward reckoned that only 5000 enemy survived and escaped and he reported that bodies were washed up and scattered all along the Flanders coast.

When he received news of the French defeat at Sluys King Philip VI is reported to have been very distressed. Indeed, for some time no one dared tell him the bad news. In the end the bearer of the bad tidings was the King's own jester: 'Oh the cowardly English, the cowardly English' he burlesqued before the King. When asked why, he replied: 'They did not jump overboard and drown like our brave Frenchmen when your Majesty's ships went to the bottom.' It was said afterwards that the fish drank so much French blood that if God had given them the power of speech they would have spoken French.

The Battle of Sluys ended the threat of French invasion of England. Ten years later it was another enemy who threatened invasion and it was again Edward who brought a Spanish force to battle and in a close run thing put the Spanish galleys to flight. The battle went by the curious name of *Les Espagnols sur Mer*.

In 1350 the scene was set for a major encounter in the Channel, for much skirmishing had been taking place between English and Spanish vessels and much ill-will had been created between these two nations. The predictable encounter occurred when a fleet of Spanish vessels sailed up the Channel to discharge merchandise at Sluys. Having accomplished this mission the force set out down Channel, prepared to meet the English should they put to sea. 'They had marvellously prepared themselves' Froissart tells us, 'with all sorts of warlike ammunition; such as bolts for crossbows, cannon and bars of forged iron to throw on the enemy . . . with the assistance of great stones, to sink him. When they weighed anchor, the wind was favourable for them: they were forty large vessels of such a size and so beautiful it was a fine sight to see them under sail.' Indeed, they must have been a fine and splendid sight, each mast adorned with coloured standards and bearers and their tops filled with men and missiles.

Edward's ships left harbour and despite the Spanish galleys being larger and faster than his force of cogs he set an intercepting course and brought the ships to battle. Edward, attired incongruously, we are told, in a black velvet jacket and a small hat of beaver 'which became him much', helped pass the time by asking minstrels aboard to play a German dance and made Sir John Chandos, who recently introduced it, sing it with them: this singing and dancing before battle displayed a sang-froid that even Drake would have found difficult to match.

The music and dancing was abruptly interrupted by the masthead lookout's call of sighting ships: 'I see two . . . three . . . four . . . and so many that God help me I cannot count them.' Trumpets were ordered to sound off and the ships to form a line in preparation for battle. King Edward ordered wine to be served to his knights after which helmets were donned—and the Spaniards were carefully scrutinized as they bore down imperiously upon the smaller English vessels: the Spaniards could have avoided battle had they so wished for they had the weather-gage—but they disdained to sail by.

Edward ordered his ship's captain: 'Lay me alongside the Spaniard who is bearing down on us: for I will have a tilt with him.' This jousting term implied an intention to ram the enemy. It was a wild decision—and it was almost disastrous. Strong and large though the cog was, it was considerably smaller and less robust than the galley. The ramming had a whiplash effect upon the Spaniard which dismasted her but so damaged the King's cog that only bailing by the knights saved the ship. Another Spaniard bore down upon the damaged cog; they grappled with chains and hooks and fierce hand-to-hand fighting ensued. Brave deeds by the Englishmen saved the day. They conquered the Spaniards and took command of the ship whose crossbowmen, Froissart recorded, 'shot such bolts of iron as greatly distressed the English'.

The Black Prince, now in his twenties, had a similar experience to that of his father. His ship suffered so many holes 'that the water came in very abundantly'. The leaks could not be stopped and despite being grappled by a Spanish ship the cog was in a sinking condition. Fortunately for the Black Prince another English ship with the Duke of Lancaster aboard secured alongside the Spaniard's disengaged side and together they captured her.

The outcome of this hard-fought battle was disputed. Certainly the English were hard-pressed and losses had been grave, but equally serious had been the Spanish losses: fourteen ships had been lost or taken and the rest of the fleet dispersed. Edward had been left in command of the sea still seeking the enemy and that by naval standards is victory. Edward's trumpeters sounded the retreat and the bloodied ships returned to England. Not inappropriately had Parliament named Edward 'King of the Sea' earlier in his reign.

Centuries were to pass before another member of the English royal family was to lead a fleet into battle—more than three centuries in fact before a royal prince commanded a fleet at the Battle of Lowestoft in 1665; but before we chronicle the adventures of James, Duke of York, we ought to take at least a sidelong glance at the Tudor sovereigns: for although none of them so much as commanded a ship let alone fought a fleet battle at sea, some of them at least exerted a profound influence upon the navy during its formative years. While Edward III had won the title 'King of the Sea', Henry VIII was called with some justification 'Father of the English Navy'.

Some credit must go to Henry's father, Henry VII for laying the foundations of a navy and all credit is due to Henry VIII for continuing his father's good work and establishing a fleet, albeit small and relatively ineffective, but he provided the climate and the opportunity for the navy to embark upon the route to sea power and command of the seas.

It is sad that Henry and his reign should have been traduced by historians, film directors, playwrights and moralists for his libertine ways and for his desperate efforts to father a legitimate male heir for the kingdom. The fact is that he straddles the stage of English history like a giant. In physical stature as a young man of twenty-nine he was described by the Venetian ambassador to England in 1519 as 'extremely handsome'.

Henry was competitive in sports and played to win. He excelled at several outdoor pursuits, wore out up to ten horses a day when hunting and played tennis skilfully. He lived and fought lustily and far from being the coarse vulgarian as he is often depicted he was one of the most cultured men in Europe. Yet, incongruously, he was also cruel, unpredictable and savagely ruthless when he thought fit.

From a navy of half a dozen or so ships at the beginning of his reign in 1509 Henry VIII expanded the fleet both in numbers and quality: by the end of the reign it comprised several score vessels of improved design, seaworthiness and armaments. Like earlier kings he also built one ship very much larger than the others. This vessel of 1000 tons was the famous *Henri Grace à Dieu* or the *Great Harry*, a monster of a ship, four-masted, with a massively high medieval fo'c'stle and aftercastle. These castles housed many guns. The *Great Harry* was, in fact, a ship in transition. She bridged the medieval design of ships with high castles from which soldiers threw down missiles upon enemy ships and grappled in hand-

Henry VIII is shown in the waist of the Great Harry, *the second ship on the right in this engraving of his embarkation for France in 1520. (National Maritime Museum)*

to-hand fighting alongside, and the coming age of naval artillery.

Heretofore the heavy guns used ashore were too weighty for mounting aboard ships' castles for they would create too much weight resulting in instability and their recoils would be too damaging to the ships' structures. It is said that Henry himself suggested the idea of mounting the cannons on the lower decks, firing through ports which could be securely fastened against the sea. It was not entirely new to shipbuilding—it had been known in the Mediterranean but it was new to England and northern Europe.

This monster of a hybrid ship underlined, nevertheless, the giant stride forward in naval architecture of this period; it enabled ships to avoid hand-to-hand fighting and to engage the enemy in battle at a distance. New tactics needed to be evolved. The *Great Harry*, thanks to Henry VIII, was a revolutionary concept in marine warfare; she gave birth to the broadside, the full effects of which were to be experienced by later royal admirals of the twentieth century, notably at Jutland and Cape Matapan.

The splendour of this great golden ship—typical of the man— should not disguise the many contributions Henry made to the growth of the Royal Navy in the sixteenth century. He established an Office of Admiralty with a Navy Office and appointed commissioners, instituted salaries for his admirals, captains and seamen and encouraged recruitment into a service that was beginning to be regarded as a profession: from this time forward England was to produce eminent naval officers in a never-ending stream. Many such seafaring officers emerged in the reign of Henry's and Anne Boleyn's daughter, Elizabeth Tudor, the first queen to give her name to an age; foremost among those seamen were Sir Walter Raleigh, colonizer of Virginia in 1584; Sir Richard Grenville who gave his life in the *Revenge* in 1591; Sir Francis Drake who, as every school child knows singed the King of Spain's beard at Cadiz in 1587; and Charles, Lord Howard of Effingham, victor over the 'Great, Noble, Invincible Armada' in 1588. Even the slightly lesser-known Sir John Hawkins and Sir Martin Frobisher, judged by any standards, towered above their fellow men.

The navy's fortunes declined during the reign of James I (VI of Scotland) to reach their nadir about the year 1620. Yet it was that same year that marked a maritime event of momentous consequences for the history of the English-speaking peoples. No Pilgrim Father aboard the humble *Mayflower* as he set foot on Plymouth Rock could have been aware of the giant ripple effect of his simple act of courage and faith.

But better things lay ahead for the navy under the Stuart kings. Charles I in an act of self-aggrandizement employed naval architect Phineas Pett and his son Peter to construct the biggest ship ever built in England. The ship's tonnage was 1637—which coincided precisely with the year in which she was launched, regarded favourably by many in naval circles as an omen of good fortune. More importantly, she outstripped all ships before her in fighting capability and majesty. She was the world's first ship with three complete tiers of guns, numbering over a hundred in all. So great was the *Sovereign of the Seas* that even the Elder Bretheren of the Corporation of Trinity House were roused to declare 'we are doubtful whether cables and anchors can hold a ship of this bulk in a great storm'.

This great ship was covered with gilded carvings, from the equestrian figurehead of King Edgar at the bows to the gilded gingerbread on the stern where Victory, Jason the Argonaut,

Hercules and Neptune were depicted. On her sides and bulkheads there was arrayed a riot of figures—gods, more than life-size females, satyrs, caryatids, signs of the Zodiac, greyhounds, unicorns, lions and dragons—set off with roses of England, thistles of Scotland and fleur-de-lys of France: along the length of the middle gun deck ran a frieze displaying guns, shields, swords, battleaxes, suits of armour, drums, muskets, flags and banners. From her yardarms streamed colourful banners: she was a ship of splendour to behold and the greatest ship the navy had ever known.

In Cromwell's time her name became shortened to *Sovereign* and after the Restoration she gained royal favour and became the *Royal Sovereign*. She saw active service during the Dutch wars in the second half of the seventeenth century and was a flagship at the Battle of Barfleur in 1692, but four years later she suffered an igmoninious fate when burnt in the Medway, victim of a fire started by a candle in a careless cook's cabin.

The *Sovereign of the Seas* witnessed some significant changes in the navy not least among which were the administrative changes during the Interregnum which helped eradicate some of the corruption and inefficiencies under James and Charles I. Commissioners appointed by Parliament now superseded noblemen favoured by the Court: army officers brought into the service as generals-at-sea injected a measure of discipline and pride. William Penn, father of the founder of Pennsylvania, commanded a ship at the age of twenty-three and was a general-at-sea at the age of thirty-two. Robert Blake, who first went to sea at the age of fifty, was arguably the greatest general-at-sea with notable triumphs over the Dutch during those long years of struggle when supremacy of the Narrow Seas was contested fiercely between Holland and England. There were a few forays further afield, such as the one when New Amsterdam was captured and renamed New York in 1664, but it was in the Channel and North Sea where the history of Europe and of the navy was being written and a sailor prince who gave valuable service both ashore and at sea was the brother of the restored King Charles II, James, Duke of York.

2

James,
Duke of York

IN THE AUTUMN of 1664 King Charles II was to be seen almost daily inspecting his ships in harbour and taking a lively interest in their preparations for war, for another clash of the two leading maritime nations seemed inevitable. Holland was still smarting—the words Pepys used were 'it will make them quite mad'—over the loss of the Cape Verde Islands and of New York. Charles had written to his sister:

> You will have heard of our taking of New Amsterdam, which lies just by New England. 'Tis a place of great importance to trade. It did belong to England heretofore but the Dutch by degrees drove our people out and built a very good town, but we have got the better of it, and 'tis now called New York

The seventeenth century was marked by unprecedently vigorous competition between England and the United Provinces of the Netherlands for overseas trade, and for mastery of the Channel and of the North Sea and the period was scarred by antagonisms and jealousies so violent that they resulted in severe clashes at sea and in three most bitterly contested wars.

The first of these Anglo-Dutch Wars broke out in 1652 after plans to form a political alliance between the English and the Dutch were frustrated. It was a brief but fiercely fought war at sea, with some of the bloodiest fighting yet seen in wartime. The war was confined almost exclusively to great battles at sea. The Dutch suffered defeat, in particular at Portland and on their home ground off Scheveningen where the Generals-at-sea Robert Blake and George Monck (later the Duke of Albemarle) and the Admirals

William Penn and John Lawson decisively routed the Dutch fleet which was driven, shattered, into harbour. The Dutch lost not only the war but the whole of their maritime trade which was now cut off by the English who commanded the Narrow Seas. They also lost their maritime pride, for in accepting the Navigation Act of 1651 they agreed to strike their flags to English ships in the Channel and the North Sea. England secured important political and economic advantages through her supremacy at sea.

But the rumblings of Dutch discontent went on unabated throughout the 1650s during Oliver Cromwell's notorious period of weakness and penury in naval administration. Although he had inherited a fleet built up by Charles I and paid for out of the unpopular tax known as ship money, Cromwell had allowed the navy to decline in the last years of his Commonwealth; resources were depleted and large debts for supplies and sailors' pay were accumulated. Samuel Pepys recorded that he thought the navy was in 'a deplorable state'.

Samuel Pepys, who was secretary to Admiral Edward Montagu, accompanied his naval cousin to Scheveningen to collect the King and the Duke of York in May 1660 for the King's Restoration. 'With a fresh gale and most happy weather we set sail for England,' wrote Pepys in his diary on 23 May, the day of their embarkation. And so Charles II returned to the throne of England to scenes of enthusiasm among the general populace and to the relief of those of higher rank. Naval commanders were prompt and strong in their immediate support of the monarchy—Monck, Penn, Lawson, Montagu and others quickly pledged their services and they were rewarded with kingly patronage. The large navy debt of £750,000 was soon paid off and sums were allocated by the King to replenish stores. Large new ships laid down under Cromwell were now quickly completed and others were refitted and modernized with heavier artillery.

Three people emerged to play an important part in the restoration of the navy's fortunes. The first of this trio was the energetic and zealous James, Duke of York, as Lord High Admiral; he relied heavily upon the experience and discretion of Sir William Penn; and completing the trio was the enterprising and devoted servant, Samuel Pepys.

A detail from Lingelbach's the Embarkation of Charles II *captured the scene at Scheveningen. (Her Majesty the Queen)*

Ever since he was a child James had borne the title of Lord High Admiral but on 16 May 1660, the eve of Charles's Restoration, he bestowed the title afresh upon his younger brother. In fact it was to be another eighteen months before James received his official commission once Charles was safely installed in his Whitehall Palace.

James had had a tough and demanding upbringing: he escaped in woman's clothing from St James's Palace where he was imprisoned during the Civil War and spent twelve years in military service on the Continent before returning with Charles in 1660. This background influenced his formative years and he grew to become a tough, efficient, obstinate man of principle with a natural aptitude for organization and a splendid mind for business. But it is only fair to say that it is doubtful if he took the initiative in most of the reforms connected with his name. Yet it is true that he was to become the ablest naval commander ever to sit on the throne of

England. And like a twentieth-century king, he never lost the slight stutter he inherited from his father.

One of the first things James undertook was to draft a memorandum setting out how the Admiralty and the navy should be regulated. The draft recommendation was finally submitted to the Privy Council under the chairmanship of the King. On 2 July 1660 it was given the stamp of approval and James set about implementing the proposals. He set up a small Navy Board consisting of a treasurer, a surveyor, a comptroller and a clerk of the acts. In addition to these, three commissioners were appointed; they had no specific duties but they were expected to devote themselves to the interests of the navy. The appointees were men of substance, widely experienced and with much to contribute to the newly constituted Board. Chief of them was Sir George Carteret who became treasurer; he was a one-time sea-boy

James, Duke of York and Albany who later became King James II. Painted by Godfrey Kneller. (National Portrait Gallery)

who rose to the position of Governor of Jersey where he rendered good service to Charles and James during the Interregnum while they were in exile on the island. Another veteran, Sir William Batten, was appointed surveyor; he was an admiral having served both the Commonwealth and Charles when he was Prince of Wales. The nominated comptroller was Sir Robert Slyngsbie, but he was soon to be replaced by another sea captain, Sir John Mennes, friend of Prince Rupert.

The appointee for the clerk of the acts was nominated by Admiral Montagu; it was his twenty-seven-year-old cousin, Samuel Pepys. It was an extraordinary appointment, not only because of Pepys's youth and also his lack of knowledge of everything naval and military: but more particularly because it turned out to be one of the most important appointments ever to be made in the interests of the navy. When Pepys realized the value of the post which his admiral patron so unexpectedly seemed to be able to offer him, he anxiously set about rectifying his ignorance of matters nautical.

The first three commissioners were John, Lord Berkeley of Stratton, a cavalier soldier and an old and trusted friend of James; Sir William Penn, the admiral who, as we have already seen, had given support to James and fought for Oliver Cromwell! The third commissioner was Peter Pett, most famous shipbuilder son of a shipwright family which for a hundred years had 'built the State's chief ships'. He was required to live in and look after Chatham Dockyard. Of these commissioners by far the most important was

Sir William Penn. He had commanded a ship in 1642, was a Commonwealth general-at-sea and was knighted with Monck and Montagu by Charles aboard the *Naseby* bringing the King back to England.

The Board thus constituted acted as an influential advisory council to both James and the King. Initially it met weekly and its principal officers were paid salaries rather than fees as an indication of the importance of the posts and as a hedge against corruption. Carteret as treasurer received £2000 a year and at the other end of the scale Pepys and Penn received a munificent £350 each. Pepys also enjoyed the fringe benefit of an official residence adjoining the new Navy Office in Seething Lane close by the Tower of London. Pepys was well aware of the bounty which had come to him. James, Duke of York and Lord High Admiral of England with his newly constituted Navy Board brought to the navy a rare and unprecedented professionalism.

Portrait of Samuel Pepys by J. Hayls. 'I . . . do almost break my neck looking over my shoulders to make the posture for him to work by,' wrote Pepys. On 16 May 1666 he paid £14 for the completed portrait and 25s for the frame. He holds a song Beauty, Retire Thou *which he had set to music. (National Portrait Gallery)*

James took his duties seriously. Samuel Pepys testified to this in his diary, and Montagu, soon to be created the Earl of Sandwich by King Charles, also spoke admiringly of James's 'application to his work'. James issued instructions to captains of warships ordering them 'to take care that Almighty God be duly served on board your ship twice every day by the whole ship's company according to the litturgy of England'. Disciplinary rules were drawn up; the forfeiture of a day's pay was to be the penalty for a sailor's cursing or blaspheming; and 'those who pisseth on the decks', he instructed, were to be lashed up to a dozen times. More importantly, James published a set of instructions for the fleet in good time for the Second Anglo-Dutch War (1665–7). These consisted chiefly of simple signalling directives and instructions for the tactical handling of ships and squadrons at sea in defence and offence, taking advantage of winds and employing fireships. He also encouraged the selection of gentlemen volunteers to serve in the navy and thereby created for the first time a volunteer reserve of naval officers.

The Duke of York and Samuel Pepys had a responsibility for the royal dockyards. This painting by an unknown artist shows East Indiamen at Deptford. In 1663 this dockyard employed 238 men. (National Maritime Museum)

James made no secret of the relish with which he anticipated a renewed outbreak of war with the Dutch, in part at least with the hope of distinguishing himself as Lord High Admiral, and when he gained the support of Parliament and—importantly—their financial backing, the clamour for war grew fiercely and James redoubled his efforts in preparing the fleet for battle. He had great confidence in his ships. He inspected them at Portsmouth and at Chatham where he boarded the 46-gun *Swiftsure*. He cruised for four days in the Channel with his friend and cousin Prince Rupert of Bavaria the experienced sea commander. It was the first time that James experienced service at sea.

By the autumn of 1664 the dogs of war had been let slip—and they continued to run till the March of the following year when war was declared again.

Pepys confided to his *Diary* on the last day of 1664: 'Publique matters are all in a hurry about a Dutch warr. Our preparations great: our provocations against them great.' Many courtiers, like James, were avid for the prospects of war and all that it entailed in the way of wealth, glory and honour. Whatever wealth, glory and honour were to be won, they would be won at sea, for the impending war was to be an entirely maritime one in which ships in enormous fleets would fight as formations in fierce artillery duels where superior cannon power would win the day. Thanks largely to the efforts of James and his administrative staff, the English fleet and organization—controlling naval stores, victualling and ship maintenance—were well prepared for war so that when it finally broke out on 4 March the fleet, as in 1914 under Prince Louis Battenberg's leadership, was to all intents and purposes ready for war. Indeed, it was already assembling at the Gunfleet, an anchorage south of Harwich opposite Dovercourt on the Essex coast.

When James joined his squadrons as Commander-in-Chief at the end of the month he was joining a powerful force commanded by professionals. The fleet was organized into Red, White and Blue Squadrons. James himself took command of the Red or Centre Squadron whose Vice Admiral was the highly experienced Sir John Lawson. He also had aboard his flagship, the *Royal Charles*, Sir William Penn as Captain of the Fleet and Captain John Harman as the ship's commanding officer. The White or Van Squadron was commanded by HRH Prince Rupert while the Blue or Rear Squadron had as its senior admiral the recently created Earl of Sandwich, Pepys's cousin, Sir Edward Montagu.

Other senior officers abounded: there were the Vice Admirals Sir Christopher Myngs and Sir George Ayscue and Rear Admirals Sir William Berkeley, Robert Sansom and Thomas Teddiman aboard the *Royal Katherine*.

The fleet which James was soon to take to sea was the largest that had ever set out from England. Penn's young son, who had been visiting his father till the landsmen were ordered ashore, counted 103 men-of-war apart from fireships and ketches, a figure confirmed by Samuel Pepys's assistant, Will Hewer, a few days later in Harwich. The fleet, in fact, comprised 109 men-of-war mounting 4192 guns, with another 28 fireships: altogether manned by 21,006 officers and men. Morale aboard the English ships—as well as ashore in England—was high, with every expectation of victory by the Lord High Admiral.

James boldly led the fleet from its anchorage on 21 April across to the Dutch coast with the dual hope of intercepting returning Dutch merchantmen and of enticing the enemy fleet to action. It was not altogether abortive. A total of eight merchant ships were brought home as prizes, captured as the fleet sailed between Scheveningen, the port for the Hague, and Texel to the north, the principal Dutch naval base. Unknown to James, the enemy fleet was not ready to put to sea for another fortnight. During this time James was obliged to take his force back to England for re-victualling—but chiefly for renewing stocks of beer! The fleet came to anchor on 15 May and it was on this day that the Dutch fleet put to sea.

The Dutch Commander-in-Chief was Jacob van Wassenaer, Baron of Obdam, described as 'a man of quality and personal courage', but he was not in the same class as Admiral De Ruyter upon whom this command should have fallen but he was at sea off Africa. Obdam, a one-time colonel of horse who was said to get seasick in a breeze, now commanded a mighty fleet. Vice Admiral Jan Evertsen was Second-in-Command. With them sailed the Admirals Stellingwerf, Kortenaer, Tromp, Cornelis Evertsen (Cornelis the Old, Jan's brother) and Schram. Each of these had

Jacobus Baro de Wassenaer, Dynasta in Odam, Suerverio, Aquilœck, Rochnœr, Lindwyck, Simow, Cyelen, & Prœfectus et Chliarchæ conscry Gubernator et futura vice aciei futropuqi, Hotlandæ propugnaculumque in actu commeavtion, Archithalaßus Hollandiæ it West-Frisiæ, Equit reg's Ordin. & Gubernator, Dux rep's item Classevsim, tribusqi officere heri, vivo virtute heroitum. D. D. D. Theodor. Matham

*Jacob van Wassenaer, Baron of Obdam,
who command the Dutch fleet at the Battle
of Lowestoft. (Rijksmuseum, Amsterdam)*

under him two junior flag officers so that the Dutch fleet wore no less than twenty-one flags. The fleet organization was extraordinarily fragmented into seven squadrons.

The presence of two Evertsens as flag officers calls for some comment. The Evertsen family had a long and distinguished association with the Netherlands navy similar to many of the proud names—Hood, Savage, Wallace, Inglefield—in the lists of the Royal Navy.

The twenty-three-year-old Cornelis, The Youngest, was already a prisoner of war in English hands. The diarist John Evelyn noted on 20 March 1665:

To White-hall to the King, who called me into his bed-chamber, as he was dressing, to whom I showed

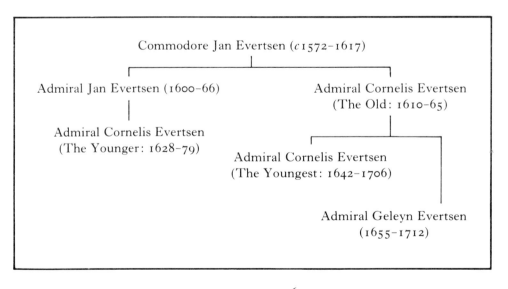

the letter written to me from the Duke of York from the fleet, giving me notice of young Evertsen . . . newly taken . . . His Majesty commanded me to bring the young captain to him.

DEN E. MANHAFTEN ZEE-HELD IAN EVERTSZ. RIDDER, VICE ADMIR.ª VAN ZEELANDT. &.

Lieutenant Admiral Jan Evertsen of the great Dutch family. (National Maritime Museum)

Four days later Evelyn wrote:

> I presented young Cornelis Evertsen . . . to his Majesty; the
> King gave him his hand to kiss, and restored him his liberty;
> asked many questions concerning the fight (it being the first
> blood drawn) . . . then I was commanded to go with him to the
> Holland Ambassador.

The Duke of York, according to Pepys, met young Evertsen the
following month. On 17 April, Pepys recorded: 'And Evertsen
when he was brought before the Duke of York and was observed to
be shot through the hat, answered that he wished it had gone
through his head rather than be taken.'

The Dutch fleet, now assembled and ready for the Battle of
Lowestoft as the engagement became known, matched almost ship
for ship, that of James's. There were 103 men-of-war and 11 fireships, mounting all told 4869 guns and manned by 21,556 men.
Morale aboard the Dutchmen was low and politics intruded to
such an extent that Obdam himself was at odds with many of his
senior officers, so that even at sea he was beset by political bicker-
ing. But soon after putting to sea he must have thought his luck was
changing when his fleet fell in with a convoy of nine English-
Hamburg merchantmen on 20 May and captured the lot. Obdam's
forces then continued towards the English coast in search of
James's fleet.

On 28 May James, still at the Gunfleet, learned that Obdam was
at sea. As the wind from the east was unfavourable to the English,
James sailed northwards for Southwold Bay where the fleet anchored on 31 May. Southwold then was a large bay capable of
providing a safe anchorage for over a hundred ships, but today the
coastline runs north-south straight as a plumb-line.

On the afternoon of 1 June the fleets sighted each other some
leagues apart and each fleet tried to manoeuvre for position, but the
wind dropped and for two days the fleets were becalmed, presenting
a splendid sight—two hundred and more ships with acres upon
acres of sails spread. On the evening of 2 June the rival forces were
only two leagues apart and battle was expected to be joined the
following day. At 2 o'clock in the morning of 3 June, when the

fleets were a few miles off Lowestoft, a southerly gale got up and according to a contemporary report, probably written by Sir William Penn himself aboard the flagship: 'At 1/2 past 3 ye wind at SSE they tacked upon us, ye fight then began by ye White Squadron . . .' This change of wind was fortunate for James, for it gave the English fleet the weather-gage, a good steady wind, a clear sky and a calm sea.

The two fleets were sailing east on parallel courses then the Dutch put about, and moving west along the line of English ships exchanged broadsides as guns came to bear on each ship in succession. The battle soon developed into a mêlée with much tacking on both sides. 'At 8' our chronicler reported, 'A signal from us [the flagship] ye Reare of our fleete tackt upon ye front of theares, at 1/2 past 8 all our fleete weare about many of our ships far asterne . . . we then held up our mainsail and bore up close to Opdam and ye *Urania.*' Obdam's flagship, the *Eendracht* of 76 guns, in the centre of the Dutch line, fought a fierce duel with James's 80-gun ship *Royal Charles*, but failed in an attempt to board the English ship. Then, two remarkable events occurred, the first described as 'At 12 came A shot from Opdam yt Kild ye Earl of Falmouth, Lord Musgrave and Mr. Boyle.'

During the height of this private battle between the rival flagships a single chain shot from the Dutch narrowly missed killing James. It killed three of his friends standing close by him: Charles Berkeley, recently created Earl of Falmouth, Lord Muskerry, one of James's Gentlemen-of-the-Bedchamber, and Mr Boyle who was the younger son of the Earl of Burlington. Blood spattered over James as he stood on the quarterdeck and he was slightly wounded in the hand by a splinter of bone from Mr Boyle's skull.

By now James's plan of fighting the battle in line had foundered; his own Squadron was in the van instead of the centre; Sandwich's Rear Squadron was in the centre and Rupert's Van Squadron was in the rear. But the private battle between the flagships continued with varying intensity until it came to an abrupt end at two-thirty in the afternoon, when the *Eendracht* blew up with a frightening explosion and sank, taking with her 404 men, including the gallant Obdam. Only five men survived her sinking. The flagship had suffered a hit in her powder room and her going was as numbing as

In this painting by van Minderhout of the Battle of Lowestoft the Duke of York's flagship the Royal Charles *is shown on the left closely engaged with the Dutch flagship the* Eendracht. *(National Maritime Museum)*

the loss of the *Hood* in battle with the German *Bismarck* in 1941.

Vice Admiral Jan Evertsen, Second-in-Command, at once hoisted the flag of Commander-in-Chief and spiritedly continued the battle, marshalling around him some twenty or more ships. But the sinking had a demoralizing effect upon the Dutch and many of their ships began to give way. Another serious blow was the death of Vice Admiral Kortenaer aboard the *Groot Hollandia*; at his death the ship's captain fled from the battle, for which he was later court-martialled, convicted of cowardice and exiled. Yet another Dutch casualty was Lieutenant Admiral Stellingwerf.

By four o'clock in the afternoon, as Vice Admiral Cornelis Tromp later reported 'the fleet got into such a confusion that they all ran away from the enemy before the wind and . . . some ships fell foul of each other and were taken or burned by the English'. James gave the signal for general chase which continued throughout that Saturday night and the following Sunday morning. The battle had become a rout. Tromp's report continued: '. . . we had . . . separated from each other in a confusing way. The next morning [Sunday] we perceived the Duke of York and Earl Sandwich astern of us and saw that we had 10 or 12 sail with us.'

Tromp, Cornelis and Jan Evertsen fought gallantly to the last. Jan Evertsen's ship suffered sixty crew members killed, his ship was holed in seventeen places and ammunition practically exhausted.

In the event, the Dutch losses amounted to thirty-two ships lost and over 6000 men killed. It was a disaster of staggering proportions for the Dutch, while conversely for James, Duke of York, it was a significant and authoritative victory.

When the defeated Dutch ships arrived in the Maas and the Texel, outraged citizens demanded scapegoats and Admiral Tromp himself entered the ring by accusing many of his ships' captains whose vessels bore no signs of battle of cowardice and infamy. Many captains were court-martialled and the outcome was that three captains were sentenced to be shot in front of the whole fleet, three others were dismissed with ignominy having had their swords broken; three more were exiled, including the captain of Kortenaer's flagship. It was an ugly episode in the Netherlands' proud naval history.

Meanwhile, James, exhausted by the bloody battle retired to the Buoy of the Nore in the mouth of the Thames having lost only two ships in battle; but losses in men killed were considerable; no less than two hundred of the *Royal Charles*'s crew had been killed.

James travelled with Prince Rupert to meet his brother the King at Whitehall Palace, there to be told that neither James nor Rupert was to return to sea during the rest of the campaigning season because of the dangers involved. In James's stead, the Earl of Sandwich was given command of the fleet.

James argued strongly to induce Charles to change his mind, but the King, no doubt influenced by James's strong-willed wife, the Duchess Anne, daughter of the Lord Chancellor, Sir Edward Hyde, and by the motherly Queen Mother, refused to concede. James remained ashore. He accepted Charles's offer of a commission to go north to put down a republican rising and in so doing avoided the worst of the Great Plague which had descended upon London from the Levant in July 1665. In September James joined his brother in Oxford where Parliament had moved for safety from the diseased streets of London. Parliament voted a further £1¼ million for the continuation of the Dutch naval war together with a personal award of £120,000 to James 'in token of the great sense they had of his conduct and bravery' at the Battle of Lowestoft.

James, still Lord High Admiral, seemed to settle thereafter into a period of relative ease and devoted himself with less than enthusiasm to his naval duties. The responsibility for the unpreparedness of the ships and defences of the navy during the Dutch foray into the Thames just two years after the Lowestoft victory in the summer of 1667 must rest largely with him.

Lieutenant Admiral Michiel Adrianszoon De Ruyter—Holland's Nelson—scored his most striking victory when he led a squadron audaciously into the Thames estuary. His squadron bombarded Sheerness, landed a force on the Isle of Sheppey and forced a passage up the Medway near to Chatham Dockyard and burned the English ships laid up there. James's flagship at Lowestoft, the *Royal Charles*, was boarded, captured and towed away virtually undamaged as an incomparable prize to the plaudits of the Netherlanders. Her heavily decorated stern is still preserved in the Rijksmuseum in Amsterdam. De Ruyter's flag and esteem never flew so high. England was humiliated. And a few weeks later England was happy enough to sign a peace treaty ending the Second Anglo-Dutch War.

James brought to his Admiralty duties in the years of 1668 and 1669 a resurgence of reforming zeal, admonishing the Board members for neglect, and instituting additional resident commissioners at Portsmouth and Harwich, a decision clearly motivated by De Ruyter's raid into the Medway. During this period, according to Pepys, James performed his duties as Lord High Admiral in a keen and conscientious manner, and it was during this period, too, that for the very first time the navy became known as the Royal Navy.

It was to be many years before James took to sea again in command of a fleet. It came about in May 1672 at the beginning of yet another Anglo-Dutch War—the Third (1672–4). During this war England had the French as her allies and it was a combined Anglo-French fleet which came under James's command. The Dutch fleet was commanded still by the legendary De Ruyter, now sixty-

Lieutenant Admiral M. A. De Ruyter (1607–76) was the Nelson of the Netherlands: a giant among the famous band of Dutch seventeenth-century admirals, he was the Duke of York's chief adversary. His striking success in the Medway in 1667 humiliated England. (Rijksmuseum, Amsterdam)

A Dutch artist's impression of the capturing of the Duke of York's flagship, the Royal Charles. *(National Maritime Museum)*

five years old but still fighting fit. His fleet comprised 75 ships-of-the-line and frigates, 36 fireships, 4484 guns and 20,738 officers and men. The combined Allied fleet under the Duke of York's command, presented a mighty challenge to De Ruyter. It comprised 98 ships-of-the-line and frigates, 30 fireships, mounting in all 6018 guns and manned by no less than 34,496 men.

The Dutch fleet was much improved in morale and skills over that which suffered rout off Lowestoft many years before. De Ruyter and his admirals had trained and exercised their ships in manoeuvres, drills and tactics to a high degree of efficiency, including the new tactic of operating ships in line, giving rise to the new name for the bigger ships—ships-of-the-line.

James's flagship was the *Royal Prince*, a brand new 1st rate of one hundred guns which led the Red or Centre Squadron; the Earl of Sandwich commanded the Blue or Rear Squadron; and the

French Squadron under the command of Admiral D'Estrees was given the honour of leading the White or Van Squadron, a curious decision considering the fact that Jean D'Estrees had been an army general until as recently as 1668.

The combined fleet was at anchor in Southwold Bay to re-victual after sortieing off the Dutch coast in search of De Ruyter's fleet. The fleet lay parallel with the coast, the French Squadron to the south, the Duke of York in the centre and Sandwich to the north. A stiff north-easterly on-shore wind provided the ideal conditions for an enemy fleet with fireships to wreak destruction. Sandwich expressed his anxiety to James at a Council of War on 27 May but the Duke dismissed the warning and fortunately for him the wind eased, so that when De Ruyter's fleet suddenly appeared early the following day James was spared the rapid assault by fireships and the cannonade of ships-of-the-line. But he only escaped a staggering defeat by the skin of his teeth.

The combined fleet had been caught at anchor with no sea-room, some men and officers still ashore, boats plying back and forth victualling and storing ships. De Ruyter was within an ace of a a brilliant victory—a victory which hung upon a wind.

The English and French ships cut their anchor cables and made frantic efforts to get under way. Sandwich led his Squadron to the NNW, towards the Dutch, quickly followed by James's Squadron in some disorder. Jean D'Estrees also got under way quickly—and headed SE—away from the enemy as if fleeing to avoid battle or perhaps to seek sea-room.

De Ruyter saw the Allied movements and despatched about twenty ships of the Zeeland Squadron under Banckerts to keep track of D'Estrees's thirty-three ships, thus shortening the odds somewhat against the English. This also had the effect of eliminating both Banckerts and D'Estrees from the main battle for they never came to grips with each other. De Ruyter advanced slowly in two divisions: in the first there were eighteen ships and thirty fireships, followed by De Ruyter himself in the centre with his main force and Van Ghent in the rear. Among his experienced captains there were Van Brakel, hero of the Medway who led the captured *Royal Charles* to Holland, Jan Van Rijn, who had broken through the protective chain across the Medway, the Youngest

During the Anglo-Dutch maritime wars of the seventeenth century half the hospital beds in England had to be set aside for the wounded from the navy. This wooden carving of a Stuart sailor is in St Bartholomew's Hospital, London. (St Bartholomew's Hospital)

Evertsen and his cousin Cornelis.

De Ruyter exploited his advantage and bore down on the disarrayed English ships. Action began at about three o'clock in the afternoon and continued for several hours until dusk, resulting in heavy casualties on both sides. The Dutch fireships in particular wrought severe damage among the English ships. Sandwich's flagship, the *Royal James*, engaged Jan Van Brakel's *Groot Hollandia* in a specially fierce engagement in which Sandwich's one hundred guns were greatly superior to Brakel's sixty. But Brakel was undeterred. His ship grappled the *Royal James* but was repulsed. He was then boarded but escaped. He went back for more despite half his crew being killed and fifty of the remainder wounded. Only the arrival of Van Ghent saved Brakel from complete destruction. Later in the evening Van Ghent was killed.

Two approaching fireships were sunk by the guns of the *Royal James*, but a third ship grappled her and the flagship was set ablaze; the fire caught hold and the ship was abandoned. Sandwich, accompanied by his son-in-law, Sir Philip Carteret, got into a crowded boat which overturned and everyone aboard was drowned. Several days later his body was recovered from the sea and it now lies buried in Henry VII's Chapel in Westminster Abbey.

Richard Haddock (later Admiral Sir Richard), Sandwich's captain, was

36

taken prisoner and later wrote to the Duke of York complaining that Vice Admiral Sir Joseph Jordan 'passed by us very unkindly to windward and with how many followers of his division I remember not, and took no notice of us at all'. The first lieutenant of the *Royal James* was also taken prisoner and put aboard the *Zeven Provincien*, and De Ruyter allowed him to watch the rest of the battle from the poop deck: from this vantage point he witnessed the battering of James's flagship.

James was obliged to shift his flag many times during the Battle of Solebay, firstly from the *Prince* whose 'main-top-mast was shot by the board, her fore topsail, her starboard main shrouds and all the rest of her rigging and fighting sails shot and torn to pieces . . .' A second shift was made to the *St Michael* and later in the afternoon to the 96-gun *London*, which necessitated spend-

A contemporary artist's view of the fiercely contested Battle of Solebay. (National Maritime Museum)

37

ing three-quarters of an hour in a long boat in the midst of battle.

By dusk both sides were exhausted by the day's battle: each had suffered fearful casualties of about 2500 dead. At nine o'clock that evening De Ruyter called it a day and withdrew his fleet towards Holland. Despite his losses he could be well satisfied: he had so mauled the English squadrons that they were immobilized for some weeks. De Ruyter had, in fact, prevented a seaborne landing of Allied troops on the Dutch coast. It was a grateful Dutch nation to which De Ruyter and his sailors returned.

For his part, James, Duke of York, Lord High Admiral of England, should have thanked his lucky stars. He could be grateful for a merciful providence which delivered him from the fireships, and which denied De Ruyter the NNE wind which then even more providentially for James veered to the SE to allow his fleet to gain sea-room; he had come within a breath of losing his fleet.

James pursued the departing De Ruyter across the North Sea but he lost track of the enemy ships in the fog and a subsequent gale. He returned to the Buoy of the Nore to lay up his ships for refitting at Sheerness and Chatham in preparation for the next year's campaigning.

The Battle of Solebay in June 1672 marked the virtual end of James's office as Lord High Admiral. The Duke's increasing conscience regarding his Roman Catholic faith prohibited him from attending Anglican services during the winter of 1672–3: he antagonized the Commons and at Easter 1673, when he refused to take Communion with the King, the diarist John Evelyn recorded that it gave 'exceeding grief and scandal to the whole nation that the heir to the throne and the son of a martyr for the Protestant religion should apostasize'.

Just before Easter Parliament passed the first Established Test Act which denied Catholics from holding any public office. Evelyn asked rhetorically: 'What the consequences of James's apostacy will be, God only knows and wise men dread.' In fact on 15 June James resigned his post as Lord High Admiral and thus ended his long association with the navy, a career distinguished by personal courage in high command at sea and by personal endeavour in high office ashore.

3

The Georgian Princes

BY NO STRETCH of the imagination could Prince Edward be described as a professional sailor. It is true that he joined the navy as a nineteen-year-old-midshipman, ostensibly to embark on a naval career, but his were days of royal patronage and it is clear even at this distance of time that Prince Edward had no intention of serving his time up the ladder of promotions. In the event, the rapid rate of promotion was a travesty.

Within five years of entering the navy as an untrained midshipman, Prince Edward—still only twenty-four years old—was Vice Admiral of the Blue* and had been appointed C-in-C of the Mediterranean Fleet. This career, with its remarkable rate of promotion, deserves at least a passing reference.

Prince Edward Augustus was the second son—born in March 1739—

The foppish-looking Prince Edward as a young man. (National Maritime Museum)

---

* At this time the navy was organized into three squadrons. In order of seniority they were Red, White and Blue, representing the centre, van and rear. Flag officers were promoted successively through Rear, Vice and Full Admiral of these squadrons.

of Frederick Lewis, Prince of Wales and his wife Augusta, daughter of Frederick, Duke of Saxe Gotha. He was a well-connected lad. His paternal grandfather was King George II and his elder brother, Prince George William, was to become George III. Only one year separated him from this elder brother so the two Princes shared their boyhood experiences and were educated together.

Their first tutor was the Reverend Francis Ayscough, whose appointment was due to his family connections rather than to his competence in teaching English history and the elements of Christianity. But his critics were probably less than fair: Horace Walpole spread the story that at the age of eleven the older boy could not read English, perpetuating the legend that they were badly educated, but letters show that by the age of eight the boys could read and write not only in English but in German as well.

Nevertheless, when Edward was ten, Ayscough was displaced by a new tutor, George Lewis Scott, 'a man of exceeding good character' and both Ayscough and Scott were responsible to Lord North, father of the future prime minister, whose post of governor to the boys earned him £1000 a year. The boys' father prescribed a demanding timetable but this was no more than was thought necessary and proper for boys' education in the early eighteenth century. Lessons started at eight a.m. and lasted till twelve-thirty: after a play hour and dinner at three there were further lessons through the long afternoon till supper at eight and bed between nine and ten.

The young Prince Edward grew into a handsome young man, attractive to the girls who understandably felt flattered when a prince of the royal blood flirted with them. But he was more than a lady's man. He had courage and spirit and this served him well when he joined the navy in May 1758 at the age of nineteen. He travelled to Portsmouth to join the 3rd-rate 64-gun ship *Essex* as a midshipman.

The navy which Edward had joined was a tough, rugged service marked by hardship and injustice for the ordinary sailor. A patriotic and jingoistic song of this time which has lasted through the centuries to this day was 'Rule Britannia', first performed in 1740, which exhorted Britannia to rule the waves to ensure that Britons would not be slaves. But an unappreciative government and nation took pains to deny the navy the ships, provisions and personnel it deserved: instead ships were manned by no more than fifteen per cent of volunteers at the time of Prince Edward's entry into the navy, the balance having to be supplemented by various means of compulsion among which the notorious press gang was the most iniquitous—and effective. Officers led parties of tough seamen ashore or to board merchant ships to seize and press into service any seamen they could lay hands on. Men imprisoned for debt were given the option of the navy or prison which prompted Dr Johnson to remark 'No man will be a sailor who has contrivance enough to get himself into a jail; for being in a ship is being in a jail with the chance of being drowned.' Vagabonds, beggars, destitute boys and foreigners—all were grist to the naval mill. The wonder is that the seamen of Britain were moulded into efficient ships' companies and fought so valiantly. They had little to fight for—except survival. They were paid a nominal amount: roughly a pound a month in the form of a ticket encashable at a cash office on Tower Hill in London, of little use to men from Plymouth and Portsmouth where ticket touts offered swingeing deductions for cash purchasing of the tickets. It needed another Pepys to eradicate the morass of corruption in the civil branch of the navy and the profiteering of unscrupulous suppliers. Just before his momentous victory at Quiberon Bay in 1759 Admiral Hawke reported that the hard ship's biscuit was 'so full of weevils and maggots that it would have infected all the bread come on board this day'.

Seamen fed on a diet comprised chiefly of biscuits, dried meat or fish—the basic victuals of the day—became subjected to scurvy and other deficiency diseases, and the awful overcrowding in dreadfully cramped quarters ensured the rapid spread of infectious diseases. It has been reckoned that during the Seven Years War of 1756–63 nearly one hundred times as many sailors died of diseases and other causes than were killed in battle.

When Prince Edward joined the *Essex* in 1758 the country had been at war with the French for two years. The main British offensive had been concentrated in the North Americas, resulting in the fall of Quebec and the conquest of Canada. In Europe, France prepared to invade England, even as Prince Edward joined the navy, and forces were being assembled in northern French ports.

Edward participated in an operation against St Malo under the naval command of Commodore Howe, destined to become the great Admiral of the Fleet Earl Howe, victor of the Glorious First of June 1794.

Prince Edward's naval service gave rise to friction between his older brother Prince George and their father. George wanted desperately to gain a King's Commission and even offered to serve as a volunteer in the army. He wrote to his father: 'I really cannot remain immured at home like a girl while all my countrymen are preparing for the field and a brother younger than me allowed to go in quest of the enemy.' At that time, Edward was aboard the *Ramilles* in a squadron under the command of Rear Admiral George Rodney, later victor of The Saints in 1782. The squadron had been sent to Le Havre to sink French invasion craft and Edward regularly wrote to his brother describing his experiences, which only seemed to inflame Prince George's jealousy.

In 1759 Edward's promotion from midshipman to post- (or senior-) captain made a mockery of royal privilege: a post of *honorary* captaincy would have been more appropriate but the height of sycophancy was reached when Edward was also given command of the 44-gun *Phoenix*, an appointment for which he was totally ill-prepared. The ship was engaged in blockade duties in the Bay of Biscay. On returning to Portsmouth in the autumn of 1759 this twenty-year-old Captain relinquished his command.

He remained ashore for over two years during which time he was created the Duke of York in April 1760. A year later he was promoted to the rank of Rear Admiral of the Blue. The following year —1762—he hoisted his flag in the 80-gun 2nd-rate ship *Princess Amelia* (named after George III's daughter) and spent the summer afloat as Second-in-Command of the Channel Squadron, commanded by the victor of Quiberon Bay, now Admiral Sir Edward Hawke. Edward's flag captain was no less a man than Commodore Howe under whom he had served as a midshipman so few years previously. The months were spent in abortive sorties in search of enemy ships. When he returned to port—promoted again to Vice Admiral of the Blue, the Duke resigned his command and remained ashore till the following year.

At the age of twenty-four he received the prestigious appointment of C-in-C of the Mediterranean Fleet. Now that peace reigned, there was no chance of action and it seems that Edward tired of the peacetime routine and resigned his command to come home. It was the end of his active service but a few years later in 1766 he received his final promotion to the rank of Admiral of the Blue.

In the August of the following year he visited the South of France, caught a chill which gave rise to complications and failed to respond to treatment. On 17 September 1767 he died. His body was embalmed, taken aboard the frigate *Montreal* and returned to England for a lying-in-state before interment in the Henry VII Chapel of Westminster Abbey. Edward Augustus, Duke of York has the rare distinction of being probably the most unprofessional C-in-C the navy has ever known and the least deserving of the rank of Admiral.

Perhaps the greatest contender for the distinction of being the least deserving of the rank of admiral was Edward's brother. Prince Henry Frederick was born on 27 October 1745, the fourth son of Frederick, Prince of Wales.

His loving mother was over-protective and personally supervized his education which he repaid by turning out to be the black sheep of the family. As a young man he chased after women and reports indicate that he often caught them. Lady Mary Coke was shocked to see him riding through Hyde Park in his carriage with a mistress by his side. 'I believe he is the first of the royal family', she wrote, 'that ever carried their mistress in the royal equipage.' Lady Craven claimed an affair with him and just before he entered the navy in 1768 Lady Sarah Banbury was his mistress.

His entry into the navy merely acted as a temporary interruption to his womanizing. His naval service, like his brother's, was a mockery. Although twenty-three years of age when he joined as a midshipman, he took nine attendants with him aboard the frigate *Venus*, commanded by Captain the Hon. Samuel Barrington. The *Venus* spent a few months in desultory sailing in the Channel, going no further than Spithead. At the end of October this junior, inexperienced midshipman was promoted captain, in command of the *Venus* superseding the poor Barrington.

Detail from a painting by George Knapton showing Prince Henry Frederick and his older brother, Prince William, playing with a ship. Prince William is shown in naval uniform although he did not serve in the navy. (Her Majesty the Queen)

A few months later in March 1769, Prince Henry, still only twenty-three, was promoted to Rear Admiral of the Blue. Captain Barrington was re-appointed, this time as flag captain to his former midshipman. Three months later Prince Henry was appointed C-in-C of the Channel Squadron as he led the squadron on a cruise to Gibraltar and back. But in October of 1769 after only four months in command, Henry struck his flag and the *Venus* was paid off. The navy was well rid of him. A contemporary, Thomas Byam Martin, recalled Prince Henry's visit to the 74-gun ship *Valiant* in company with his nephew Captain Prince William: 'I remember a conversation taking place respecting the dimensions of the *Valiant's* masts and on some reference made to the mizzen mast, the gallant admiral asked which was the mizzen mast. The Duke was a man of very small intellect.'

Prince Henry reverted to chasing women. In 1770 Lord Grosvenor claimed damages of £10,000 and named Henry in an act of criminal conversion, the eighteenth-century expression for adultery. Henry had to ask the King for a large loan to pay the damages and costs. In the following year Henry contracted a morganatic marriage with Ann Horton, a twenty-seven-year-old widow, two years older than Henry. She was the daughter of Simon Lutterell, Lord Irnham, head of an old Irish family and described as 'the greatest reprobate in England'. The marriage became the jest of London. But worse still, the marriage was made without the King's approval and the King refused to recognize his brother's wife as a member of the royal family. An announcement was made that those who paid court to the Duke and Duchess would not be received by the King and Queen. The King made sure this would never happen again: the Royal Marriage Act of 1772 made it necessary for the Crown's consent for any marriage by a member of the royal family.

In October 1770 Prince Henry received promotion to Rear Admiral of the White and a week later to Vice Admiral of the Blue. Despite his loss of favour at court he was further promoted to Vice Admiral of the White in 1776, ironically, making him senior to the great Admirals Rodney, Keppel and Howe. In 1778 he was promoted Admiral of the Blue and four years later to the navy's most senior rank at that time, Admiral of the White.

Prince Henry, profligate Duke of Cumberland, the admiral who knew not his mizzen from his main mast, died in 1790, leaving nothing but an exiled widow and masses of debts.

4

Prince William, Duke of Clarence

Prince William Henry was born on 21 August 1765 between three and four in the morning at Buckingham House in London. He was the third son in a row of King George III and his consort, the young and plain Princess Charlotte Sophia of Mecklenburg-Strelitz. It was not regarded as an event of great significance at the time for no one could know that the baby prince would one day inherit the throne of England as William IV. Horace Walpole commented at the time: 'If it were not for the Queen, the peerage would be extinct. She has given us another duke.' Queen Charlotte was to do much to preserve the peerage. Her prime function was to ensure succession to the throne by the supply of a sufficiency of male children. She and her royal husband applied themselves assiduously to this task and in the first twenty-two years of their marriage she was to bear George III nine sons—and six daughters for good measure.

First born was George Augustus Frederick, later Prince of Wales and King George IV; Frederick Augustus, later to become Duke of York and Albany, followed a year later. These elder children and William were brought up in tranquil and decorous surroundings at Richmond, then later at Kew in what was then the Dutch House, now known as the Queen's House, which still survives within the precincts of the famous Kew Gardens.

William's education was shared with his younger brother, Edward, at a house on Kew Green there to be 'put into the hands of Governors' for a period of seven years. Chief among the tutors was a Hanoverian Major-General by the name of Budé supported by Henry Majendie, summoned from Christ's College, Cambridge.

For the next few years the lives of the two young Princes,

William and Edward, were to follow an ordered and sequestered routine under the redoubtable Majendie supported by a dancing master, a fencing master, riding masters and writing masters.

The boys absorbed Latin and Greek with ease: they were less happy with French and while William's grasp of arithmetic had its limitations he developed a sense for mathematics.

King George III took a lively and sincere interest not only in the education of his sons but also in their career prospects. Prince George, the eldest son, Prince of Wales, and already at the age of sixteen, a young profligate, was destined for the throne. Prince Frederick, the future Duke of York, and the second son, would embark upon a military career. What then would become of a third son? Clearly, William had little prospect of inheriting the crown, and his father gave deep thought before deciding upon the navy as William's career. William was later to declare that nothing had made him happier than the decision by his father to make him a sailor.

Before despatching the thirteen-year-old to sea, King George sought the advice of several naval acquaintances including Rear Admiral Robert Digby and the Commissioner for Portsmouth Dockyard, Sir Samuel Hood. The latter provided the King with a shopping list of clothing and gear which William should bring along with him:

3 dozen Shirts and Stocks
2 Hatts and 2 round ones
2 dozen Hand Towels
Pocket Handkerchiefs, night caps or Netts, Basons, Washballs, Brushes, Combs etc.

On 15 June 1779—it was the day before war with Spain was declared—midshipman the Prince William Henry with 'a hair trunk, two chests and two cots done up in a mat' arrived at Spithead to report aboard Rear Admiral Digby's flagship, the line-of-battle-ship of 98 guns, the *Prince George*. Prince William recorded the event faithfully in his log book still preserved two hundred years later in the National Maritime Museum, the first of three red leather-bound and gold-tooled volumes, maintained with scrupulous attention to detail:

His Royal Highnefs
PRINCE WILLIAM HENRY, their MAJESTIES third Son,
in his Naval uniform, on board the Prince George.

Prince William with Rear Admiral Digby aboard the Prince George. *'He was a fine-looking youth with a florid complexion, light hair and a pleasing countenance, but of a squat form.' (National Maritime Museum)*

Winds N. Light airs and fair. Moored at Spithead. I came from Ken with General de Budé at about twelve, found at Sir Samuel Hood's, Lady Hood, Admiral Darby, Mr and Mrs J. Hood. At one Admiral Digby carried me on board, I went to every part of the ship where I was received with universal joy . . .

William was also accompanied, incongruously, by the Reverend Henry Majendie, as midshipman and private tutor extraordinary, who bore carefully detailed instructions from the King as to the Prince's education. Instruction was to be offered 'my dearly beloved son . . . in the Christian religion, to inculcate the habitual reading the Holy Scriptures'. English composition figured large in the curriculum and Majendie was instructed to correct spelling and style in William's letters home but not to tamper with the sentiments. History, Latin, French —'a language now become so universal'—were to form part of the lessons. Majendie shared with the Prince the hardships of living in the crowded confines of the midshipmen's mess. A Captain Chamier described a typical midshipmen's mess of this time: midshipmen, he recorded

dressed and undressed in public; the basin was invariably of pewter; and the wet towels, dirty head [lavatory] brush etc were, after use, deposited in his chest. A hammock served as a bed, and so closely were we all stowed in war, that the side of one hammock always touched that of another; fourteen inches being declared quite sufficient space for tired midshipmen.

King George was particular in his instructions to Sir Samuel Hood. On 11 June 1779 he ordered: 'The young man goes as a sailor, and as such, I add again, no marks of distinction are to be shown unto him; they would destroy my whole plan.' But such instructions were incapable of implementation: the King's son could not, in fact, be treated exactly as every other midshipman for nothing could disguise the fact that he was of royal blood and colleagues instinctively treated him if not with respect or reserve, at least as someone different.

Furthermore, although William shared the duties of cooking in his mess—including stealing the flour to powder his hair when he dined with the admiral—he was a frequent dinner guest of the admiral's. The admiral's steward meticulously recorded the day's menus in his day book now preserved in the National Maritime Museum. One entry records: 'Boiled ducks, smuthered with Onyons. Purtatoes, French Beans, carits and turnips. Beackon. Albacore [fish]. Fruit Friters with whipt cream. Spanish Friters. Boiled Beef and Rst Mutton.' It would be easy to say that such meals made the transition from palace to the gunroom bearable but it is only fair to say that the young prince took to his new life much as other teenage midshipmen—with reasonable conscientiousness, sometimes getting into trouble, fighting and cursing. He shared the hard life of being at the beck and call of the first lieutenant, working with the seamen to learn the trade, climbing aloft for sail work, keeping watches and manning boats. William was developing into young adulthood in a reasonably normal way. The navy always was a good leveller.

But Thomas Byam Martin saw it differently:

The sort of respect, ceremony and submission shown to a boy of the Prince's age [sixteen] by my father and other official elders quite astonished my young mind, and made me think it could scarcely be a human being to whom so much adulation was due

The King put it to his son in a letter rather differently:

Though when at home a Prince, on board the *Prince George* You are only a Boy learning the Naval Profession; but the Prince so far accompanies You that what other Boys might do, You must not. It must never be out of Your Thoughts that more obedience is necessary from You to Your Superiors in the Navy, more Politeness to Your Equals and more good nature to Your Inferiors, than from those who have not been told that these are essential to a Gentleman

These words of advice make strange reading today, and one wonders how HRH Prince Philip expressed his advice to his sons Prince Charles and Prince Andrew on their leaving the family home to join the Royal Navy.

After a brief spell of leave at Windsor over Christmas-tide 1779 William rejoined the re-victualled *Prince George* for a six months' cruise, in the course of which the young Prince was to experience his first taste of action. The French had agreed to assist Spain in the recapture of Gibraltar from the English and Admiral Sir George Rodney, a sixty-one-year-old irascible and haughty aristocrat, was directed to reinforce Gibraltar, by then closely invested by the Spaniards. Rodney sailed from Plymouth on 19 December 1779 with a strong squadron of fifteen ships-of-the-line from the Channel Fleet, five more destined for the West Indies and nine frigates. This squadron gave cover for a fleet of transports for the relief of Gibraltar and a convoy for the East Indies. The force included the *Prince George* under the command of Rear Admiral Digby, and with Prince William aboard.

At daybreak on 8 January 1780 Rodney's ships sighted the Spanish force

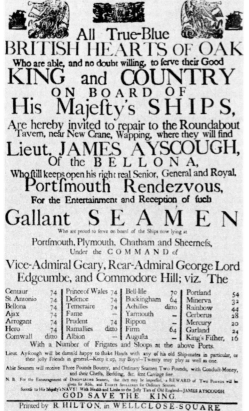

This recruiting poster dates from about the time that Prince William joined the navy in 1779. (National Maritime Museum)

Opposite Top *A portrait of* Sovereign of the Seas *and Peter Pett, son and assistant to Phineas Pett her builder and designer. (National Maritime Museum).* Bottom *The Duke of York's flagship, the* Royal Prince. *She was typical of her time, decorated with heavy gilt 'gingerbread' on the stern. (National Maritime Museum)*

south of Cape Finisterre. It comprised the 3rd-rate 64-gun *Guipu-scoana* commanded by Commodore Don Juan de Yardi, six frigates and a convoy of sixteen merchantmen bound for Cadiz with wheat and naval stores. In the ensuing chase every ship of the Spanish force was captured and the enemy flagship was renamed *Prince William* 'in respect for His Royal Highness,' Rodney later reported, 'in whose presence she had the honour to be taken'.

Rodney's fleet, including Digby's *Prince George*, resumed course and on 16 January rounded Cape St Vincent. At noon, when twelve miles south of the Cape, enemy ships were sighted and Rodney's ships crowded on all sail and gave chase before a strong westerly wind. The value of coppering ships' bottoms became evident as the greater speed this afforded the English ships enabled them to bring the slower enemy ships to battle. As the Spaniards were being overhauled they were identified as Don Juan de Langara's Squadron of eleven ships-of-the-line and two frigates. They were outnumbered two to one. Battle was joined at about four p.m. when Rodney's leading ships engaged the enemy's rear and almost immediately the 70-gun *San Domingo* blew up with a frightening explosion. Prince William described it in a letter to his father: 'A most shocking & dreadful sight. Being not certain whether it was an enemy or a friend, I felt a horror all over me . . .' Only one man from the crew of about six hundred was saved but he soon died of his wounds.

Darkness descended and the battle continued throughout the stormy moonlit night giving rise to the name 'The Moonlight Battle'. The English superiority told and by daylight Langara's flagship, had been taken along with another five 70-gun ships, the *San Julian, San Eugenio, Monarca, Princessa* and *Diligente*.

Don Juan de Langara later visited Rear Admiral Digby aboard the *Prince George* where Prince William was introduced to him. When the Spanish Admiral was preparing to leave HRH appeared and respectfully informed the Admiral that the barge was ready. Don Juan exclaimed in surprise: 'Well does Great Britain merit the empire of the seas, when the humblest stations in her navy are filled by princes of the blood!'

A curious feature of this famous naval battle was the fact that the triumphant Admiral Rodney spent the whole time confined to

Opposite *Prince Rupert of Bavaria, cousin of King Charles II and of James, Duke of York. This splendid portrait is thought to be by John Lely. (National Portrait Gallery)*

Middle-Deck of the "Hector", Man of War.

*Card-playing, dancing and entertaining women and families aboard was accepted when ships were in harbour and regarded as 'out of discipline'. This Rowlandson drawing dates from the time when Prince William was a teenage midshipman. (**National Maritime Museum**)*

his cabin with gout, an affliction which signally failed to affect his handling of the battle.

After the victory the *Prince George* sailed to Gibraltar where William and his midshipman friend Lord Augustus Beauclerk made his first trip ashore, explored the Rock and even became involved in a drunken brawl with soldiers, ending up in the local jail. Only the persistent intervention of Admiral Digby earned the boy an early release.

On its return to England in February the *Prince George* squadron fell in with a French convoy and took the flagship with her hoard of £100,000 in coins. It was a rewarding end to a thrilling cruise for the Prince. He wrote to his father excitedly: 'Thus far in the year 80 everything has been successful on our side, as if Providence was resolved to punish our enemies for having begun the war so unjustly.'

On 8 March William recorded in his log:

Had the great happiness of presenting to the King the Colours taken from the *Prince William, St Julian* and *Prothee*, the first Spanish and French Ships of the Line taken this war; & of which I was a spectator. His Majesty received them from me with great pleasure.

The people of London responded to the victory joyously and

when William visited Drury Lane a near riot more reminiscent of a modern-day pop concert with fainting girls, led to a bridge being thrown between pit and stage to allow hero-worshippers to escape. Ballads were composed, poems written and young William's praises sung by all and sundry. No one was left in doubt that he was London's popular hero.

Prince William resumed his naval service after this heady adulation with cruises of two or three months until January 1781 when, still aboard the *Prince George*, he accompanied Admiral Digby to North America where it was thought the young Prince might just help revive the flagging morale of the Loyalists. Certainly his arrival in New York was the cause of some celebration by enthusiastic crowds at the quayside. High-ranking Officers and a Captain's Guard with Colours greeted him and he met Benedict Arnold who had deserted to the British only the previous year. Prince William was not specially impressed by the New York of 1781. He wrote to his father: 'The town is built in the Dutch way, with trees before the houses. The streets are in general very narrow & very ill-paved.'

In November 1781 William transferred to Admiral Hood's flagship HMS *Barfleur* at New York where, following the disastrous surrender of General Cornwallis at Yorktown, Virginia, New York was the only remaining British base left in the north and it was here that an outlandish incident occurred. An American revolutionary, Colonel Ogden, one of General Washington's staff officers, proposed a commando-style kidnapping of both William and Admiral Digby from New York. George Washington responded enthusiastically:

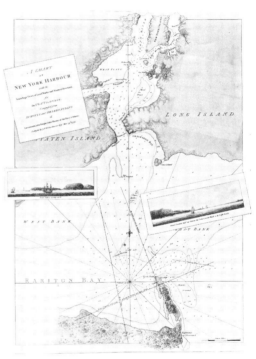

It was while serving on the North American Station that Prince William visited New York. This chart of 1779 is by the famous cartographer Des Barres. (National Maritime Museum)

The spirit of enterprise so conspicuous in your plan for surprising in their quarters and bringing off the Prince William Henry and Admiral Digby merits applause; and you have my authority to make the attempt in any manner, and at such time, as your judgment may direct.

I am fully persuaded that it is unnecessary to caution you against offering insult or injury to the persons of the Prince or Admiral, should you be so fortunate to capture them . . .
Given at Morris Town this 28th day of March 1782.
G. Washington.

But details of the plan were leaked and the operation was aborted.

In the spring of 1782 William transferred to HMS *Warwick* under the command of Captain Keith Elphinstone, who later became Lord Keith, and in this frigate he saw action off the Delaware River against the French 40-gun frigate *L'Aigle* and the 22-gun ship *Sophie*, but this temporary secondment to the *Warwick* probably cost him the chance of taking part in one of the decisive naval battles of the period—the Battle of the Saints in April 1782.

Presently Lord Hood (the former Sir Samuel) wearing his flag in the *Barfleur* arrived with his squadron to relieve Admiral Digby of both his command and responsibility for Prince William. One of his first acts was to dismiss the virtuous Majendie who was sent packing to England and to replace him by a Captain Napier. But it was an ill-fated appointment: the Prince and the Captain never hit it off. The unhappy relationship stumbled along till early 1783 before Napier, too, was sent packing.

During 1782 Prince William first met Horatio Nelson, then a twenty-four-year-old captain of the 28-gun *Albermarle*, as the future victor of Trafalgar clambered from his gig to board the flagship *Barfleur*, off Staten Island. William, as midshipman of the watch, manned the side and saluted Nelson by the gangway. 'He appeared to be the merest boy of a captain I ever beheld,' William was to write later, 'and his dress was worthy of attention. He had a full laced uniform, his lank, unpowdered hair was tied in a stiff Hessian tail of an extraordinary length.'

Both young men experienced a genuine rapport and Nelson

wrote of the Prince: 'He will be, I am certain, an ornament to our service. He is a seaman . . . with every other qualification you may expect of him; but he will be a disciplinarian . . . with the best temper and great good sense, he cannot fail of being pleasing to everyone.'

From the North American station the *Barfleur*, with William aboard, visited the West Indies where Nelson also transferred and assumed the duty of looking after the Prince for a spell. The cruise ended with the return of William to England in mid-1783 and this also marked the temporary end of his naval service. His log book petered out in mid-Atlantic and the final entry reads: 'The reason I did not continue my Log till we arrived at Portsmouth was because nothing worth mentioning happened. We arrived on the 27th of June: the ship was immediately paid off, and my name was put upon the Queen's Books during my absence in Germany.'

Two years, in fact, were spent in Hanover to acquire a courtly polish not available in a midshipmen's mess, although it is fair to say that the Prince had developed well in the navy's care if that man of letters, Horace Walpole, is to be believed; after meeting William in July 1783 he described him as: 'Lively, cheerful, talkative, manly, well-bred, sensible and exceedingly proper in his replies'.

William regarded the time spent in Hanover as squandered and in due time he received news of his recall to the navy ecstatically. He submitted himself to a meeting of the full Board of the Admiralty presided over by Lord Howe on 17 June 1785 and received his promotion to lieutenant. Howe declared that William 'was every inch a sailor' and even William's bitterest critic would have conceded that he had earned his promotion.

He hurried to Portsmouth to join—as Third Lieutenant—the frigate *Hebe*, captured from the French under extraordinary circumstances. In 1779, just three years before William's appointment to the *Hebe*, a founder, John Robert Melville, working at the Carron Company in Scotland, cast a new piece of ordnance. It was shorter than a 4-pounder and lighter than a 12-pounder, but it fired shot weighing 68 lb. It became known as the 'carronade'. Several smaller pieces were cast to carry shots of 24, 18 and 12 lbs. The Admiralty

Portsmouth dockyard and the Common Hard in the late eighteenth century. The ship-of-the-line in this engraving is HMS Victory *before her Trafalgar victory in 1805. (National Maritime Museum)*

and Board of Ordnance approved these new weapons—though the latter regarded the conventional long gun as the superior weapon—and had some fitted to ships, but naval officers were reluctant to approve them, preferring the long gun to the greater destructive power of the carronade.

In an effort to resolve the issue the navy made available the 44-gun frigate *Rainbow*, commanded by Captain Henry Trollope, for trials. She was equipped with 48 carronades in place of her traditional weaponry with a broadside weight of metal totalling 1238 lbs, whereas her former long gun broadside totalled 318 lbs. The *Rainbow* sailed in search of an enemy ship to test out her new armament. It was to take four months before she encountered a large French frigate, the 1063 tons *Hebe*, mounting 38 guns, with a crew of 363 commanded by the Chevalier de Vigney.

At seven a.m. the *Rainbow* opened fire with her bow chasers—two 32-pounders. The French Captain concluded from the size of shot coming aboard from these bow guns that the maindeck batteries would be terrifyingly larger. He exchanged a single broadside with the *Rainbow* for the sake of honour and promptly hauled down his flag! The one broadside from *Rainbow's* 68-pounders had shot down the foremast, smashed the wheel and killed one officer and four seamen. Vigney was right, his ship would have been shot to pieces in a matter of minutes; the *Rainbow's* broadside from 48 carronades was nearly four times the weight of that from the *Hebe's* 38 long guns. This action went far to establish the reputation of the carronade in the navy. And the *Hebe*, as was the custom of the day, was repaired and taken into service in the navy.

William served in her under the captaincy of Edward Thornborough on the Home station for a little under two years before managing to persuade his father of his readiness for a command of his own. After a long harangue William won his way and on 10 April 1786 he was promoted captain of the 28-gun frigate *Pegasus* and three months later he took her to the Americas. At St John's, Newfoundland, he thought 'the face of the country is truly deplorable'. Placentia he considered no better. But Halifax—and its women—he found 'very gay . . . lively . . . and . . . most obliging'.

It was about this time that his sister wrote of him: 'He is as happy as the day is long . . . the *Pegasus* is his whole delight and pleasure. He has a little Band of Musick that serves to make his ship's company dance and he says "I doat to see my men happy".'

The *Pegasus* sailed south to the West Indies where she joined a squadron commanded by Captain Nelson, then captain of the *Boreas*, enabling Prince William to resume the genuine friendship they had formed. There is no doubt that Nelson was more than content to have William in his squadron. 'Our prince is a gallant man,' he wrote. 'He is, indeed, volatile but always with great good nature. There were two balls during his stay and some of the old ladies were mortified that HRH would not dance with them . . .' Nelson went on: 'In his professional line he is superior to near two thirds . . . of the list: and in attention to orders and respect to his superior officers I hardly know his equal.' He continued in the same letter: 'The *Pegasus* is one of the finest-ordered frigates I have seen.'

By all accounts William ran a tight ship. He was a stern disciplinarian, having a seaman thrashed with the cat-o'-nine-tails for late-

Floggings aboard ship were common. In this story-picture George Cruikshank, illustrator of Dickens, shows a man confessing his guilt and declaring the innocence of the man lashed to the grating. The ship's company is mustered to the right, officers on the left, armed marines on the quarterdeck. The boatswain and surgeon stand behind the grating. (National Maritime Museum)

ness. He would spend a night ashore drinking and whoring till three in the morning yet be on deck at seven criticizing his officers for their slovenly turnout and denouncing their scandalous and disgraceful laziness, ruling that their hammocks should be taken down and properly lashed by six bells in the morning. He required his midshipmen to wear 'White breeches so tight as to appear to be sewn upon the limb . . . a pigtail of huge dimensions dangling beneath an immense square gold lace cocked hat . . .' but the breeches were apt to burst whenever the mid had to climb the rigging.

Yet he displayed a kind-hearted philanthropy and paternalism towards his own men, such as pulling strings to secure the release of a man unjustly accused of obstructing a Customs House official. On another occasion he complained bitterly that the food supplied to his ship was 'Mouldy, Rotten, Rancid, Stinking and unfit for men to eat'.

He was no easy taskmaster. Brutish, ill-tempered, afflicted by rheumatic pains in his side and thigh, undergoing a so-called 'mercury cure' for venereal disease, his strictness, one biographer records, amounted almost to torture. It was William's unrelenting discipline which involved him in a distasteful affair which marred his naval career. His first lieutenant aboard the *Pegasus* was Isaac Schomberg, a capable officer, twelve years senior in service to William and a protégé of Lord Hood's who had privately asked Schomberg to keep an eye on the young captain.

Like so many incidents, this one had small beginnings: William Hinstone, a seaman, and William Madden, a marine, were punished by the Prince for hanging up their clothes to dry between decks. Schomberg opposed the punishment. He also overruled the captain's order to punish midshipmen for hanging their wet clothing in the mizzen rigging. Both incidents underlined the personality clash which was being fanned by the unbearable climate and the deplorably uncivilized living conditions. Theirs had been a history of opposition and confrontation. Nelson first detected disharmony between the two in December 1786 and in conversation with William surprised the Prince by asserting he had a high opinion of Schomberg.

In January 1787 William threatened Schomberg with a court martial but settled for his first lieutenant apologizing before his fellow officers. Further offences—and apologies—followed until Schomberg defiantly demanded a court-martial; but on being arrested he apologized once again and urged William to forget all about it. But Schomberg was released and sent home to England where Lord Hood, now C-in-C Portsmouth, promptly appointed him First Lieutenant of the *Barfleur*, giving tacit backing to Schomberg's cause. When Nelson, too, showed bias towards Schomberg's case and then Lord Howe, First Lord of the Admiralty, heaped burning coals of discontent by criticizing William's harsh treatment of his third lieutenant aboard *Pegasus*, Prince William was in despair. 'Much as I love and honour the navy,' he wrote to Lord Hood,

'I shall beyond doubt resign if I have not a satisfactory explanation from both your noble lordships.' It was not the sort of letter to commend a young captain to Their Lordships.

This unhappy affair was relieved in March 1787 by Nelson's marriage to the widow Mrs Frances Nesbit, niece of the President of the Council of the island of Nevis, at which Prince William, somewhat to Nelson's embarrassment, insisted upon giving away the bride. 'Poor Nelson,' he recorded, 'is head over heels in love. I wish,' he added presciently, 'that he may not repent the step he has taken.'

By the autumn of that year William was at Quebec and within weeks the *Pegasus* had sailed suddenly for England, summoned probably on the instructions of the King to whose notice had come news of William's involvement with a woman. William himself viewed the summons gloomily . . . 'with a certainty that my Christmas box or New Year's gift will be a family lecture for immorality, vice, dissipation and expense . . .' he predicted. But he was probably involved with the wife of John Wentworth, the surveyor-general at Halifax. She was an American with whom the Prince was thought to be captivated—the rare but powerful attraction of a young man for an older woman. William visited her and stayed at her home frequently, giving rise to gossip. It is likely that to prevent a scandal, William was hastened home to England where he arrived on 27 December 1787.

For the next two and a half months William resided at the home of a wealthy Devon merchant named Winne (variously spelled in all its permutations) in Plymouth's Fore Street. He fell violently in love with Sally, the merchant's daughter. Later he tried to secure the post of Agent Victualler at Plymouth for Mr Winne: 'His character . . . will bear the strictest enquiry . . .' he wrote. The days in Plymouth were spent working aboard ship or in the dockyard but evenings and nights were for enjoyment and carousing, and when Nelson and his wife visited the Prince it was to witness revelry late into the night with officers lustily performing country dances in the Long Assembly Rooms. Nelson eulogized over the young Prince again. But the good living came to an end and on 13 March 1788

William and his crew transferred to another frigate, the 5th-rate, 32-gun *Andromeda*, a ship in the Channel Fleet.

Within a short time the King posted the *Andromeda* to the Americas because of William's entanglement with Sally. On hearing of William's affair in Plymouth he is reported to have declared 'What! William playing the fool again? Send him off to America...'

The *Andromeda* sailed in July 1788 and exactly one month later arrived at Halifax, 2700 miles from the Lizard. With almost indecent haste, William spent the first night ashore at the house of Mrs Wentworth but by all reports she had formed a new attachment and William seemed content to leave matters as they were. His eight month stay in Halifax was a period of almost unmatched debauchery. It started off with a bad example. When he paid his first official call on his Squadron Commander, William found Captain Charles Sandys drunk and unconscious in bed. William described him with some disgust as 'a vulgar, drunken dolt'. Nelson wrote of him two years earlier 'Between Bacchus and Venus he is scarcely ever thoroughly in his senses.' Drinking orgies became commonplace: on one occasion twenty guests including the governor, a general and the commodore consumed sixty-three bottles of wine. Parties were held aboard the *Andromeda* when William became outrageously drunk. One notorious party to celebrate the King's birthday included the firing of a salute of 160 guns; such was the noise and the jollifications that a ship in distress and ablaze five miles away firing off signals, foundered with all hands with no attempt at rescue.

Loveless relations abounded and a fellow officer recorded that the Prince would go into any house where he saw a pretty girl and that he was familiar with every brothel in town. In a moment of self-disgust William wrote 'I am sorry to say that I have been living a terrible debauched life of which I am heartily ashamed and tired.' He resolved to turn over a new leaf as he sailed *Andromeda* to the West Indies but as soon as he made a landfall his resolve evaporated and he embarked upon more drunkenness and philandering. It is only fair to balance the scales by recording that contemporary reports continued to impress that the life of dissipation in no way affected his efficiency as a commanding officer, that his ship was well handled, his crew well trained and his officers well dressed.

William's service in the West Indies was brought to a premature end by the illness of his father whose symptoms of insanity were probably due to the disease porphyria, which would account for his talking to trees and other manifestations of madness. The *Andromeda* arrived at Spithead on 29 April 1789 and three days later William was at Windsor. But he did not receive the coveted appointment at the Admiralty that he was eager to have, and the honour which was bestowed upon him—that of the royal Duke of Clarence and Earl of St Andrew in Scotland and of Earl of Munster in Ireland—ironically virtually brought an end to William's active service in the navy that he loved.

Their Lordships of the Admiralty saw no future for the twenty-four-year-old officer, no captaincy of a ship-of-the-line, no future command of a squadron, even less a fleet. Nor conversely could the Duke be confined to the command of a frigate. It is sad that this young profligate, a loud-mouthed drunkard and boor, should have been abandoned in this fashion for he had many redeeming and likeable qualities and talents which were never allowed to develop.

There was a final flourish a few months later early in 1790 when a minor war threat with Spain developed and William was recalled temporarily to command a 74-gun ship, the *Valiant* (whose namesake Prince Philip, Duke of Edinburgh, was to serve in at the Battle of Cape Matapan in 1941) and for several months the fleet was to exercise in the Channel dispirited, poorly manned, lacking in discipline. It was an unhappy time for William and when the time came for an end to his temporary command he was glad to get ashore and take up his life with Mrs Jordan. By the year end William had been promoted to Rear Admiral of the Blue.

William had met Mrs Jordan in the spring or early summer of 1790, soon after his release from the navy after a brief spell of living with a Miss Polly Finch; Mrs Jordan was then an established actress of great beauty, born Dorothy Bland in 1761. At the age of nineteen she had changed her name to Mrs Jordan, borne three illegitimate children by her lover, Richard Ford, and had reached a peak in her profession as a comedy actress—while still only a teenager! By the beginning of 1791 the Duke of Clarence and Mrs Jordan were living together openly and unashamedly. It was a liaison that was to last for twenty years, in the first thirteen of which

La Promenade en Famille. — a Sketch from Life.

Mrs Jordan is shown learning her stage lines, while the Duke pulls a
perambulator crammed with some of their illegitimate children in this
cartoon by Gillray. (British Museum)

Mrs Jordan was to bear the Duke ten children—five girls and five
boys—all of whom survived to adulthood and most of whom subsequently made satisfactory marriages.

Meanwhile, the French Revolution had erupted in violent blood-
shed claiming the head of Louis XVI and in 1793 France declared
war on England. Prince William, promoted to Rear Admiral of the
Red on 1 February, hoped for a naval command, but permission
for William to serve afloat was refused. A year later on 15 March
1794 William wrote to Their Lordships entreating them for a
command:

> Conscious that during my naval career I never committed an
> act which could tarnish the honour of the flag under which it was
> my pride and honour to fight, I solicit in this hour of peril to my
> country that employment in her service which every subject is

bound to seek, and particularly myself, considering the exalted rank which I hold in the country and the cause which it is my duty to maintain and defend . . . If the rank which I hold in the navy operates as an impediment to my obtaining the command of a ship without that of a squadron being attached to it, I will willingly relinquish the rank under which I had formerly command of a ship and serve as a volunteer on board any ship to which it may please Your Lordships to appoint me.

This heartfelt appeal failed to draw even the courtesy of a reply and another appeal to his father was equally valueless. As a sop William was promoted to Vice Admiral of the Blue and in July 1794 to Vice Admiral of the White. William accepted defeat and turned to the solace and comfort of the less capricious Dorothy Jordan and took to studying naval history. While he did so he was denied participating in some of the great naval battles of history: in 1794 there was Lord Howe's great victory over the French at The Glorious First of June; in 1797 there was Admiral Jervis's magnificent victory at Cape St Vincent where Commodore Nelson distinguished himself; there was Admiral Duncan's fight at Camperdown and Nelson's victory in Aboukir Bay. William was not comforted by the regularity of his promotions—to Vice Admiral of the Red on 1 June 1795; to Admiral of the Blue on 14 February 1799; to Admiral of the White on 1 January 1801.

During all these years William and his family—all his children bore the surname Fitzclarence—lived in Clarence Lodge at Richmond, then in apartments at St James's Palace, and finally in Bushy House. It was a handsome but unostentatious country home set in the middle of a park only a mile from Hampton Court and it was to delight the Duke for thirty years, where he was content to live the life of a farmer and watch with love, affection and an over-indulgence, the upbringing of his children. But after twenty years the lengthy love affair with Dorothy Jordan ended in a long drawn-out wrangle and a sordid financial settlement.

1811 was also the year of William's promotion to Admiral of the Fleet, the senior officer of the navy.

He hoisted his flag at sea in 1814 at the restoration of the monarchy to France, and Louis XVII returned from his exile in England in the yacht *Royal Sovereign*, with William commanding the escort squadron in the frigate *Jason*.

The second opportunity came in June of the same year when the Emperor of Russia and King of Prussia visited England to celebrate the allied victory over Napoleon. Part of the celebrations included a review of the fleet at Spithead where William's flagship, the 98-gun *Impregnable*, captained by the Hon. Henry Blackwood, one of Nelson's captains, and the rest of the fleet presented a magnificent sight. Rear Admiral Thomas Byam Martin, a flag officer with the fleet who was one of William's midshipmen aboard the *Pegasus* and *Andromeda*, was one of the many naval friends William was pleased to meet again. Martin recorded an embarrassing moment during the day when the Prince thundered at a bungling fore topgallant man manning the yards. Martin reported '. . . whereupon HRH who had been before pretty vehement in the use of a speaking trumpet, sent forth at the unfortunate man the most tremendous volley of oaths I ever heard; it quite made one shudder to hear such blasphemy.' The Prince Regent was much amused by the incident and turned to Lord Melville, the First Lord of the Admiralty, and said 'What an excellent officer William is!' It had been a great day for the Admiral.

By 1818, after years of searching among the wealthy ladies of England and the princesses of Europe, and of political manoeuvrings to preserve dynasties, the ageing Duke of Clarence was found a wife. William wrote to his eldest illegitimate son: 'It is to be the Princess of Saxe-Meiningen, whose beauty and character are universally acknowledged. She is doomed, poor, dear, innocent young creature, to be my wife.' Lady Granville described her as 'a small well-bred, excellent little woman'.

The twenty-five-year-old Bavarian Princess Amelia Adelaide proved to be an ideal wife for the fifty-two-year-old Duke who specially warmed to her endearing trait of accepting the Duke's large family with not just a dull recognition but with a genuine enthusiasm and affection. The marriage took place in July 1818 and it was to be a happy alliance but alas, not blessed with the male heir that all parties hoped for.

In 1827, now in his sixties, and after a break of nearly forty years with the navy, William was offered unexpectedly the post of Lord High Admiral, nominally a titular appointment but as we have seen, William was not one to act simply as a figurehead. He lost little time in hoisting his flag in the *Royal Sovereign* and sailed on an unauthorized cruise. On his return he peremptorily summoned the Admiralty Board to attend him at Portsmouth, rousing the members' anger, especially antagonizing the effective First Lord, the obstinate Sir George Cockburn, whom William thought as fit to be at the Admiralty as his grandmother. Sir George was so affronted that he took the matter to the Prime Minister and the King. The latter wrote to his brother, taking the Board's side un-equivocally: 'You are in Error from the beginning to the end,' he wrote decisively. 'This is not a matter of Opinion but a matter of fact.' The Board added emphasis to the argument by threatening to resign *en bloc*.

William reacted in character—in an act of thumbing his nose— he put to sea again without authorization and this time he took a squadron of warships with him for good measure. It was an act of deliberate affront and deservedly drew forth a reprimand from the King. In August 1828, William, Duke of Clarence, resigned the proud office of Lord High Admiral of England which he had held for only fifteen months. His tenure of office should not be judged by these indiscretions for he had devoted himself most assiduously to affairs of the navy. He initiated gunnery training exercises; he overhauled the promotion system; he restricted the use of the lash; he instituted regular reports on ships' battleworthiness and gunnery trials and perhaps most progressively, he sponsored the introduc-tion of HMS *Lightning* the first steam vessel in the navy.

William has been much maligned by historians and it would be folly to describe his contributions to the navy during his office of Lord High Admiral as great but equally it would be unkind to dis-miss his achievements as insignificant and him as Sailor Bill. All told, he could claim to have spent fifty years in the navy of which nearly eleven years were spent on active service in peace and war. It is an enviable record and William served the navy well.

On 26 June 1830, King George IV died and William, Duke of Clarence, inherited an uneasy crown at the age of sixty-five. Queen

William IV, the Sailor King, aboard his royal yacht in 1830, the year of his accession to the throne. Greenwich Palace can be seen in the background. (National Maritime Museum)

Victoria wrote an appropriate footnote to a letter, referring to her uncle, King William IV: 'Whatever his faults may have been, it was well known that he was not only zealous but most conscientious in the discharge of his duties as a king. He had a truly kind heart and was most anxious to do what was right.'

William IV may not have been a great king, but he was a bluff, good-hearted patriot and nursed a great affection for the Royal Navy. He had the common touch and genuinely enjoyed the affection in which he was held by the populace—and he would have accepted as a tribute the name later given to him, the Sailor King.

5

Prince Alfred, Duke of Edinburgh

ON 6 AUGUST 1844, just seven years after the Sailor King's death, a fourth child—a second son—was born to the young Queen Victoria and her consort, Prince Albert of Saxe-Coburg and Gotha, at Windsor Castle. The baby was christened Alfred Ernest Albert but to the end of his life he was to be known affectionately as Affie by his mother and father.

Alfred showed an interest in the navy from a very early age but it was unlikely that he had been influenced by his great uncle's declaration 'There is no place in the world for making an English gentleman like the quarterdeck of an English man-of-war.' Alfred also enjoyed the wholehearted support of his parents. The Prince Consort wrote to his brother, Duke Ernst II of Saxe-Coburg-Gotha, about Alfred: 'As regards his wish to enter the navy, this is a passion which we, his parents, believe not to have the right to subdue. It is certainly not right to break the spontaneous desire of a young spirit . . .' When this letter was penned in 1857 Alfred's own decision to enter the navy was already a year old and his parents had taken the decision to educate their two eldest sons privately and separately—in Alfred's case, in preparation for the navy as a career, and in the case of the heir, 'Bertie', in preparation for military service.

It was the middle of August 1858 when Alfred suffered the three-day ordeal of the examination. His parents had been on a visit to Germany and on their return to Dover they drove by coach to Portsmouth where the Commander-in-Chief, Sir George Seymour, informed them of Alfred's having passed the examination and having received his appointment to the *Euryalus* which was already on its way to Osborne. When the Queen and Prince Albert disembarked at Osborne's private pier young Alfred was there to greet them half blushing with excitement and his own success, looking uneasy in his new jacket, cap and dirk. 'We felt very proud,' Prince Albert wrote to his brother, 'as it is a particularly hard examination.' So proud was Prince Albert that he wrote to the Prime Minister, Lord Derby, enclosing the examination papers with the comment 'He solved the mathematical problems almost all without fault, and did the translations without a dictionary.' Lord Derby replied with a light-hearted touch: 'I could not but feel very grateful that no such examination was necessary to qualify Her Majesty's Ministers for their offices, as it would very seriously increase the difficulty of framing an administration!'

Prince Alfred, as a young man, is shown here in the uniform of a sub-lieutenant. (National Maritime Museum)

Prince Alfred enjoyed a spell of leave with the family at Balmoral in the autumn of 1858 before rejoining his ship. HMS *Euryalus* was a screw-steam frigate armed with fifty guns, launched only five years previously and was typical of a ship of this transition period, for the navy was entering upon the second half of the nineteenth century, a time which saw Britain enjoying undisputed mastery of the seas and embarking upon a huge programme of shipbuilding.

In December 1860 the launching of the world's first ocean-going warship with an iron hull, the 9210-ton frigate HMS *Warrior*, at Blackwell marked the start of a great arms race which was to last to this day; the changes and improvements in ships and their equip-ment was such that almost as soon as they were put into service they were obsolete. Some years later W. E. Gladstone was to say 'The fashion in ships of war is as fickle as that of ladies' hats.'

Prince Alfred was to be a witness of much of this exciting modern-ization programme and his young relations, Prince George (later

King George V) and Prince Louis Battenberg (later the First Marquess of Milford Haven) were all to experience the pride of serving in the most powerful and prestigious navy in the world. Prince Alfred took to this new life like a duck to water and once he had surmounted the homesickness on his first voyage, he settled into the ship's routine while on passage to Malta.

The commanding officer of HMS *Euryalus* was Captain John Walter Tarleton, described as a good and careful officer who had distinguished himself while in command of the 40-gun frigate HMS *Fox* in the second Burma campaign of 1851-2, when he led a small squadron of steamers up the Irrawaddy to surprise the enemy. He was now taking his new command to join the Mediterranean Fleet whose C-in-C, Admiral Fanshawe, had been instructed, like Tarleton, to accord the young Prince no special treatment aboard ship, but this constraint did not apply ashore. Indeed, the pro-gramme of visits arranged for the *Euryalus* looked suspiciously like a carefully designed and politically motivated social round of visits to the Mediterranean ports.

During 1859 *Euryalus* visited Marseilles, Alexandria, Tunis, Algiers, Malta and the Levant, including a brief tour of the Holy Land. But it was Valetta—the first major port of call—that set the pattern for the subsequent visits and when it all came to the atten-tion of the *Times* aroused an angry leader.

When HMS *Euryalus* entered Valetta's Grand Harbour it was to the accompaniment of a royal salute fired by warships and the guns of Fort Angelo. The governor's barge brought Sir John Pennefather alongside: he was resplendent in full dress and cocked hat and he brought with him an invitation for the young Prince to attend a banquet in his honour at the Auberge de Castille that evening.

The fourteen-year-old cadet Prince was driven along narrow, steep streets of cheering Maltese to meet the Island's Council, Maltese and foreign dignitaries of the church and judiciary. The *Times* in a moment of unaccustomed criticism of royalty launched into an attack on the incident: 'Prince Alfred . . . was greeted by the slogan "Viva Alfredo" by the Maltese. But why not "Viva Mr Midshipman Easy"?' the leader writer admonished pompously. 'We want him to learn his profession—not in a vapid, half-and-

Opposite Top *A midshipman's gunroom such as the Georgian Princes would have known. The junior mids messed in the gunroom under the fatherly eye of the gunner : the older ones—and some could be middle-aged—lived in the cockpit on the orlop or lowest deck. The painting is by A. Earle. (National Maritime Museum).* Bottom *Prince Henry Frederick, Duke of Cumberland, and his Duchess portrayed by Thomas Gainsborough. (Her Majesty the Queen)*

half, Royal Highness, kind of way. He was sent to be trained to salt water and it is upon rose water that his first lesson in navigation is taking place. What has a Middy to do with royal receptions and royal salutes and royal fiddle-faddles of every description?' (The references to midshipman were wrong, of course: Alfred was still a cadet.)

Queen Victoria was not at all amused. She wrote to Princess Victoria, Alfred's sister, on 1 January 1859 from Windsor Castle. 'The impudent *Times* thought fit to disapprove of his being properly and loyally received,' she observed.

It was to be another year before Alfred passed his examination for midshipman and during that time he progressed well in the *Euryalus* in the Mediterranean where England avoided being drawn into the sudden outbreak of war between Emperor Francis Joseph of Austria and Sardinia with the support of Francis Napoleon III. Early in June Napoleon and King Victor Emmanuel entered Milan and at the decisive Battle of Solferino on 24 June the French suffered devastating losses. It was at this battle that Lord Mountbatten's grandfather, Major-General Prince Alexander of Hesse and the Rhine, led his division. When Prussia threatened to come to Austria's aid, France sought a compromise peace at Villa-franca and was given Nice and Savoy as the price of her alliance. So alarmed was Britain at what Napoleon would do next that Parliament readily voted one million pounds to accelerate the navy's conversion to steam power. Had Britain been embroiled in the war Alfred's position was clear: 'Should there be war,' his mother had instructed, 'he must remain and do his duty like every other officer. I should not wish him to do otherwise.'

In February 1860 the *Euryalus* was sailed for home after more than a year's commission abroad during which time Alfred had grown in stature and graduated in the hard school of naval service.

Of his confirmation at Easter the Queen wrote: 'The ceremony went off extremely well ... To see the young sailor inured to life, its trials and hardships, its dangers and temptations, who had been in foreign lands and to the Holy Sepulchre itself, standing there before the altar was very moving to a fond mother's heart.'

Alfred was to fulfil his mother's hopes of becoming distinguished for he had chosen a career in which he was to rise to high rank

Opposite Prince William as a captain in the navy painted by Martin Archer-Shee. (National Portrait Gallery)

Prince Alfred was to rise to the top of his profession. He is shown here, near the end of his career, as a full Admiral. (National Maritime Museum)

chiefly due to his own professional efforts and personal merit.

No true assessment can be made of a prince's promotion in the navy. Any judgement as to his true worth must be assailed by doubts of privilege and favour. Nepotism, without doubt, attended James, Duke of York, and his naval appointments; William, Duke of Clarence, enjoyed benefits from his royal status though in his case they were more harshly earned; Prince Alfred was perhaps the first of all royal princes serving in the Royal Navy to progress through the ranks largely on personal merit and he was soon to be joined by his nephew Prince George. In the final analysis, perhaps a simple but true test to apply as to ability is the appointment to command a ship, for this is the appointment where any lack of ability is cruelly exposed: the Royal Navy demands complete professionalism in its commanding officers.

Alfred was a long way from command yet; he rejoined the *Euryalus* when she had completed her refit and sailed for the South Atlantic to visit Rio de Janeiro before proceeding to Table Bay in South Africa, then a vital sea port in the Empire, for a round of ceremonial duties.

Euryalus entered the beautiful bay on 24 July and one of the first visitors to clamber aboard the frigate was the harbour master. He was greeted aboard by none other than HRH Prince Alfred as the duty midshipman. The following day Alfred was accompanied ashore to Cape Town where crowds cheered and applauded as Alfred met the governor, Sir George Grey. This was the start of a long series of official receptions and functions over a period of many weeks which included visits to the recently created Orange Free State, to Algoa Bay on a cruise with the Governor to carry out ceremonials ashore in Port Elizabeth, to Natal and then back to the

Cape Colony where Prince Alfred attended the opening of Cape Town's new public library. Sir George referred to the recent cruise where colonists and native chiefs had all expressed surprise at the son of the Queen and Empress holding the insignificant rank of midshipman. 'In their eyes,' Sir George declared at the library's opening, 'the most admirable of the many things they saw was the sight of a number of hardy barefooted lads assisting at daybreak in washing the decks, foremost among them in activity and energy was the son of the Queen of England.'

In September Alfred performed yet another ceremony at almost the identical time as his older brother in faraway Canada who was opening a bridge across the St Lawrence, a situation which gave special pleasure to their father, Prince Albert. Alfred's duty was the laying of the foundation stone of a breakwater in the harbour of Cape Town. In fitting style Alfred trundled a wheelbarrow of stones to the water's edge as a symbolic start to the breakwater's construction.

By November of this year Alfred was home again to the delight of his mother who lost little time in writing from Windsor Castle to the King of the Belgians:

> Here we have the happiness of having our dear Alfred back . . . who gives *very* interesting accounts of his expedition and has brought back *many* most interesting trophies, splendid horns of *all* these wonderful animals . . . He is grown though very *short* for his age . . . He is really such a dear, gifted, handsome child . . .

But Alfred never reached the high degree of excellence his mother wished for him. Culturally he developed a deep interest in music, became an excellent violinist and took a prominent part in establishing the Royal College of Music but he also developed into the least agreeable of all the English princes, unsmiling and unpopular: his own daughter later described him as 'this strange, taciturn prince'.

In the new year Alfred was appointed to the 2nd-rate 90-gun screw-steamship, the *St George*, under the command of Captain the Hon. Francis Egerton, which was soon despatched to the North America and West Indies station where Rear Admiral Sir Alexander Milne was C-in-C. At the end of the year the Prince Consort contracted a fever and languished for days before dying of typhoid. Alfred was recalled from America but he arrived too late to see his father. After the funeral he stayed at Osborne to try to comfort his distraught mother who now embarked upon a lifetime of mourning for her lost consort. Alfred rejoined the *St George* which by now had transferred to the Mediterranean and he was still serving there towards the end of 1862 when King Otto of the Hellenes abdicated and the throne of Greece was offered to Alfred. In a plebiscite of the nation Prince Alfred won overwhelming acclaim with 230,000 votes; the second choice scored 2300; a brother of the Princess of Wales only managed to attract six supporters and Garibaldi a mere three; four French nominees each registered one vote. Alfred viewed the honour with alarm and in the event the crown went to Princess Alexandra's brother, Prince William George of Denmark, then an eighteen-year-old naval cadet, who duly became King George I of Greece.

Early in 1863 Alfred passed his examinations for lieutenant 'brilliantly' and was appointed to the steam corvette *Racoon*. She was a 22-gun ship of 1476 tons and for the next three years she was to be Alfred's home, cruising throughout the Mediterranean in the course of which she visited Spain, Italy and Greece.

A change from naval routine occurred in 1867 when it was decided that Alfred should attend a course of study at Bonn University and from there he frequently took the train journey along the Rhine valley to visit his sister, Princess Alice, second daughter of Victoria. On 24 May 1854 she had married Louis, eldest son of Alexander, Prince of Hesse and Princess Julie, created Princess of Battenberg in 1858. It was at their Schloss Heilingenberg at Darmstadt that Prince Alfred met the Battenberg children including the thirteen-year-old cousin of Louis, also named Louis Alexander. This youngster was specially impressed by the stories about the Royal Navy, the world's greatest navy and by the absurdly young twenty-three-year-old naval officer with his handsome goldbraided uniform decorated with orders on his chest. After a while the teenage Louis expressed his wish to join the navy and when Alfred heard of this he announced that he was about to commission the frigate *Galatea* and was going round the world. 'I shall be the

Prince Alfred's first command, the frigate HMS Galatea, *seen here among the icebergs in southern waters during her tour of the world in 1868. (National Maritime Museum)*

captain,' he declared proudly to Louis, 'and you must come with me.'

After completing his three-year commission in the *Racoon* Alfred returned home to a harvest of decorations: to begin with he was accorded accelerated promotion to Captain on 23 February 1866. Presently he was granted a personal income of £15,000 and created the Duke of Edinburgh and Earl of Ulster and Kent. He was awarded the Freedom of the City of London, and Trinity House elected him its Master. His loving mother bejewelled him with orders but it was a later award which pleased him most. On 22 January 1867 the Admiralty appointed him to HMS *Galatea* 'in command'. These words of magic to a naval officer brought to Alfred those same feelings of pride of achievement experienced by all officers given their own command. The *Galatea* was a 3227-ton screw frigate capable of 13 knots. She had been launched ten years earlier and was now to embark on a shakedown cruise to the Mediterranean prior to a world tour to allow Alfred to undertake a long list of ceremonial duties. The first of these was performed in Lisbon where the King of Portugal dined aboard the frigate hosted by the twenty-three-year-old captain Prince.

Alfred's arrival in Valetta's Grand Harbour must have been a daunting experience. As the most junior captain joining the station he was aware of the critical watch maintained by all other ships' commanding officers as he came in to anchor the *Galatea*.

After a brief spell the *Galatea* left Gibraltar for her world cruise. Rio de Janeiro, the first port of call, was a foretaste of what was to come at every port: receptions, balls, dinners, luncheons. The Emperor and Empress dined aboard the British ship and Alfred was entertained lavishly ashore. This contrasted strangely with the more simple fare provided by the islanders of Tristan da Cunha where the tiny unnamed village on this sparse, barren, volcanic island was christened with the name Edinburgh in honour of Alfred.

The awesome beauty of the Cape of Good Hope became visible to the crew of the *Galatea* on the fine morning of 15 August 1867. Among the many official duties were the pleasanter naval occasions when he visited his old ship *Racoon* now attached to the station and HMS *Petrel*, recently having landed the Dr Livingstone search party at the Zambesi estuary. The visit was also marked by Alfred's laying the foundation stone for a new graving dock—'a dock capable of holding the largest ships in Her Majesty's navy'—a ceremony accompanied by much colour and jubilation. The highlight of the visit to South Africa was the series of elephant hunts which gave Alfred great pleasure.

The long haul from the Cape to South Australia took in the expected spell of heavy weather—'the ship was scudding under close-reefed topsails and reefed foresails, before terrific squalls through a high, mountainous sea'—before the *Galatea* steamed into Adelaide harbour to the acclamation of the crowds assembled to witness the first royal tour of Australia. It was the greatest day in Adelaide since the day thirty-one years before when the first governor landed on the Mount Lofty plains and took possession of them in the name of Alfred's great-uncle, King William IV.

Melbourne (which ten years prior to the Duke's birth was a trackless forest), Hobart in Tasmania, Brisbane and Sydney all responded enthusiastically to the young Duke. But on his second visit to Sydney it nearly all came to a grisly end in an assassination attempt.

A contemporary report says that 20,000 Australians assembled at the Yarra Street Wharf in Geelong to see Prince Alfred when he made the first royal tour of Australia. (National Maritime Museum)

Two British ships other than the *Galatea* were in harbour—the *Challenger* and the *Charybdis*—under the command of Commodore Rowley Lambert. Crews from these ships were attending a fête and picnic ashore in aid of the Sailors' Home at Clontarf, attended by the Governor, Sir Alfred Stephen, by the Earl and Countess of Belmore and by Alfred himself. It was 12 March 1868. After lunch, the Duke was strolling, in conversation with local magnate Sir William Manning, when an assassin pushed his way forward, followed the Duke for a short spell then fired a pistol at his back. Alfred collapsed, exclaiming 'Good God! I am shot. My back is broken.' The bullet, its impetus arrested by the thick joint of Alfred's braces, nevertheless penetrated the back, missing the vertebral column by half an inch, on a level with the ninth rib and lodged in the flesh within two inches of the breastbone.

Herbert James O'Farrell, the would-be assassin, fired a second

77

shot—at Manning—but the pistol misfired. A coach-builder named Vial and numerous sailors overpowered the assailant and they were prevented from lynching him by a host of policemen who hauled O'Farrell off to a ship for his own safety. He was an Irishman with Fenian-terrorist sympathies who was greatly dismayed by his failure to kill the Duke. 'I have made a mess of it,' he lamented, '. . . I am sorry I missed my aim. I am a Fenian. God save Ireland!' He died by hanging on 21 April.

Alfred made a good recovery at Government House but the assassination attempt aroused meetings of indignation throughout Australia expressing horror and resolutions of undeviating devotion to the Queen. Alfred reassured the Australians: 'The cowardly act of one individual has not, in any degree, shaken my confidence in the loyalty of the people of this colony towards the throne and person of Her Majesty.'

The tour was brought to an end and the *Galatea* was sailed direct to Portsmouth via the Horn and she arrived at Spithead on 26 June 1868 after an absence of seventeen months.

The interrupted tour was reinstated the following year and Alfred became the first member of the royal family to visit Hong Kong, and the sub-continent of India where he arrived in December 1869. Here he experienced the munificent entertainment of the local native rulers who vied with each other during the Duke's stay of three months.

At the end of this Far Eastern tour the *Galatea* finally paid off early in 1872 and Alfred attended a gunnery course before going on to half pay while awaiting a further command. It was to be another four years before his naval career resumed and during this time he became engaged to the only daughter of Tsar Alexander II of Russia, the twenty-one-year-old Grand Duchess Marie Alexandrovna. The wedding took place in June of 1874 and over the years the parents were blessed with five children, perhaps the most interesting of which was the second born, Marie, who became the mother of King Charles II of Roumania and the grandmother of King Peter of Yugoslavia. On his marriage, Alfred had the rank of honorary captain in the Russian navy conferred upon him.

The 1870s were an exciting period of naval history and Alfred was to be both a spectator and a participant in some of the innovations and developments, both in the gradual evolution of the ships in the fleet and in the conditions of employment of seamen and officers. In the late 1860s the royal gun factories had produced a new type of muzzle-loading gun which provided the navy with a reliable weapon—until the breech-loader was perfected many years later. In ship design, the Admiralty was blessed with enterprising naval architects who rose to the challenge thrown down by the needs of gunnery. With the passing of sail, steamships enjoyed greater freedom of manoeuvre which necessitated more flexible patterns of fire than the rigid broadsides of the wooden walls. The revolving armoured turret with wide arcs of fire went a long way to solving this problem, but this desirable feature required the turret to be mounted on a ship's upper deck to achieve all-round fire. Thus, sails, masts, rigging—all had to go—and the transition to steam propulsion was accelerated.

In 1873 there came the revolutionary HMS *Devastation*. She was the first sea-going turret ship without sails or rigging. She symbolized decades of technological evolution, as dramatic as the appearance of the first nuclear-powered submarine. She displaced 9330 tons, had a bunkerage of 1800 tons of coal, with engines capable of propelling her at nearly 14 knots. More importantly, she carried four 12-inch rifled guns in two turrets mounted fore and aft with great arcs of fire. The battleship was being born and would continue to develop into the magnificent ships of the twentieth century until air power would bring the battleship era to an end.

The 1870s saw development too in the torpedo invented by a Mr Whitehead in 1866, and a special design of ship, the *Polyphemus*, was brought into service mounting five torpedo tubes. As early as 1872 the commanding officer of HMS *Excellent*, the naval gunnery school, formed a new branch which taught the mechanics of torpedo warfare. In charge of this branch was Captain J. A. Fisher. He predicted that 'the issue of the next naval war will chiefly depend on the use that is made of the torpedo, not only in ocean warfare, but for the purposes of blockade'. The use of the torpedo in the U-boats' unrestricted warfare of 1914–18 proved the truth of this prediction. By the end of the decade the navy's first torpedo boats were in service and they attended the naval review in the Solent in 1878.

The Mediterranean Fleet at Malta. HMS Sultan *is clearly visible at anchor left of centre. On the far right is the famous* Devastation, *the first turret ship in the navy without sailing masts. The Italian artist*

Another class of warship to emerge during this period was the high-speed, heavily armoured cruiser, exemplified in HMS *Shannon*, in which her designer, believing in attack rather than defence, concentrated on the cruiser's armament at the expense of armour, sacrificing much protection in favour of speed and powerful weapons. The *Shannon* was not a complete success for she had too many inherent faults but she was the forerunner of a new class of ship and even of the light or 'protected' cruiser developed at the end of the decade. The *Comus* class of eleven ships was the result of years of evolution in ship design, but these cruisers bore another distinction: they were the first ships to be constructed for Royal Navy service in the new material, steel.

The Duke of Edinburgh's next appointment—again in command

Gianni also captures the navy boats and the Maltese dghaisas. *(National Maritime Museum)*

—was to HMS *Sultan*. She symbolized much of the transitional designs of the decade. She had been built six years earlier at Chatham. She displaced 9290 tons, carried a crew of six hundred, and her engines could achieve a speed of 14 knots. A notable feature of many warships' design was their ram bows, and the *Sultan* class was designed to give ahead-firing and to combat this menace she mounted four 12½-inch MLR (muzzle-loading rifled) guns capable of ahead-firing. Her main armament comprised eight 18-ton MLR guns.

For a few months after joining her, Alfred worked her up in the Channel Fleet, before steaming to the Mediterranean to join the strong British fleet which comprised eight huge ironclads including the revolutionary HMS *Devastation*, four lighter ships of the emerging 'cruiser' class and many lesser vessels.

Developing unrest in the Balkans in 1875 simmered and boiled for some years: Bosnia, Hertzgovina, Bulgaria, Serbia, Montenegro, Turkey and Russia were all embroiled in oppression and massacre, in brutal repression of a revolt condemned by Mr Gladstone as 'the Bulgarian Horrors'. Russia, for long harbouring resentment at Turkey's control of the narrow exit from the Black Sea to the Sea of Marmara, coveted Constantinople which guarded this narrow canal like a sentinel, possession of which would provide Russia with an ice-free port and access to the broad seas of the warm Mediterranean. The political centre of gravity in the Mediterranean shifted to the east, to the Aegean, and it was in that direction that the Commander-in-Chief, Vice Admiral Phipps-Hornby, led his fleet early in 1877 through to Constantinople. After two false starts the fleet weighed anchor on 13 February at Belsika Bay in Anatolia, close to the plains of the ancient city of Troy and eight miles from Cape Hellas.

The fleet comprised *Alexandra* (flag), *Agincourt*, *Sultan*, *Swiftsure*, *Temeraire* and *Achilles*; all ships cleared for action and steamed into the teeth of a gale and a swift current. It was an inauspicious start to a delicate operation. The straits were forced with no response from the old guns of Cape Hellas. Chanak was the danger, where the narrowest neck of the straits lay under a battery of 12-inch Krupps guns. Before reaching this battery, driving snow engulfed the fleet blanketing the scene as effectively as London smog—and reminding all captains of loss by collision of HMS *Vanguard* with the *Iron Duke* in poor visibility only a few years earlier in the Irish Channel with dreadful loss of life. No effective fog-signalling procedure had been adopted since except a rule of thumb which saved the day this time in the snowy Narrows of the Dardenelles. The fleet was proceeding in two columns of three: each rear-most ship reduced speed to Dead Slow—about 4 knots—then the centre ships, then the leaders. In this fashion the ships proceeded against a 2-knot tide at a funeral speed towards Chanak; it was a five-hour ordeal in freezing conditions with leadsmen heaving the lead almost ceaselessly. At 14.30 when the snow had subsided it was to reveal the flagship aground on a shoal about a mile south of Chanak. Phipps-Hornby had ordered the Duke of Edinburgh in

Sultan to anchor and stand by. HMS *Achilles*, commanded by one of the navy's most distinguished naval officers, Captain Sir William Hewitt VC, was ordered to press on with the remainder of the squadron.

The snow descended again and Hewitt led the squadron through the narrowest neck of the channel, passed the forts unseen, and into the open waters leading to Gallipoli where the ships anchored except for *Agincourt*, commanded by Rear Admiral Commerell—another VC—who was detached back to assist the Admiral. The flagship *Sultan* and *Agincourt* safely extricated themselves from their predicament and joined the rest of the squadron off Gallipoli on the morning of the fourteenth and Phipps-Hornby led the squadron across the Sea of Marmara to Constantinople.

The political events in the Balkans with the British stance unashamedly anti-Russian aroused a lot of excitement and resentment in England which the Great MacDermott expressed in a music hall song:

> *We don't want to fight,*
> *But by jingo, if we do,*
> *We've got the ships, we've got the men,*
> *We've got the money, too.*
> *We've fought the Bear before,*
> *And while Britons shall be true*
> *The Russians shan't have Constan-ti-no-ple.*

Phipps-Hornby's passage of the Dardenelles to provide protection for the Turkish Sultan Abdul Hamid and his capital was a creditable feat of seamanship and it seemed churlish of the Sultan to refuse to parley with the English. The British ships thus embarked upon a long drawn-out waiting game anchored within sight of the Sultan's palace, while diplomats and politicians from Russia and the Great Powers negotiated a peaceful settlement. It was to take fourteen dreary months with the British ships cooped up in the Sea of Marmara maintaining a presence, cruising never more than a few hours steaming from Constantinople. Even the Congress of Berlin (June–July 1878) which brought the war to an end, brought no relief for the British ships which were compelled to wait until the last Russian troops were withdrawn from the vicinity of Constantinople nearly a year later.

Throughout this long period the Sultan maintained one of his capital ships—the British-built *Messoudieh**—secured close by the palace landing steps as a refuge in case of the need to leave in a hurry. His admiral aboard the ship was Hobart Pasha, still in the Navy List as a captain, but this diplomatic difficulty was probably no more embarrassing than the Duke of Edinburgh's captaincy in the Russian navy and Lieutenant Louis Battenberg's family connections with the Russian court.

What did cause some embarrassment in diplomatic, family and naval circles was an incident with lurid accusations in the press of the Duke allowing spies into HM ships. One of the officers aboard the Duke's ship was Lieutenant Prince Louis of Battenberg—the young lad whom the Duke had first met as a nine-year-old at Schloss Heilingenberg at Darmstadt. Prince Louis' elder brother, Captain Prince Alexander (Sandro), was a serving officer in the Russian army. The brothers met and Prince Louis invited him aboard the *Sultan*. The Duke of Edinburgh approved, and Sandro, in fact, not only stayed aboard for two days but met Admiral Phipps-Hornby aboard the *Temeraire* and even watched some fleet exercises including defence against night torpedo attacks.

When this story got out the British Press had a field day. It levelled accusations of allowing a German-born Russian officer aboard British ships at a time when these ships were engaged in helping prevent a Russian attack on Constantinople. The incident displayed at worst poor judgement and indiscretion by the Duke, both the Princes and the C-in-C, but even the Queen came close to branding Alfred a traitor. In a letter to him she described his actions as 'most injudicious and imprudent'. She went on:

Alexander Battenberg may be very discreet and no doubt is very honourable, but *how* can *you* think that the *officers* and *men* of our Navy and the Fleet of which you are a Captain will *ever believe*

---

* She was torpedoed in the Dardenelles by the British submarine *B 11* on 13 December 1914 in a daring escapade which earned Lieutenant N. Holbrook the VC.

that the *important secrets* will not be divulged? Anyway, will they ever trust you and Louis Battenberg? I will give you credit for its being an act of *extreme thoughtlessness* but that for a Captain in command of a ship, that Captain the Sovereign's son and at *such* a moment, when we don't know if we may not very soon be at war, is a very serious thing . . . Louis Battenberg's prospects will be seriously injured by it and I don't see how he can or ought to continue to serve in the same ship with you.

Press calls for the Duke to be relieved of his command and for Louis Battenberg to be returned to England in disgrace went unanswered. As often happens, the incident was aggravated by official reaction: the Admiralty rather absurdly transferred the Duke from command of the *Sultan* to command of the *Black Prince*, virtually swapping crews and sailing the *Sultan* for Portsmouth. Alfred was thereby allowed to remain in command of a ship in the Mediterranean but apparently to have been dismissed his ship, and as time passed the affair blew over. The Queen's anger was assuaged, the press and the Admiralty dropped the case and like the Turco-Russian emergency, it just faded away. At the end of the year the *Black Prince* was despatched home and the Duke appeared to have suffered little from the incident, for on 30 December the Admiralty recommended to the Queen that HRH the Duke of Edinburgh, 'having now served at sea as captain in command of your Majesty's ships for a period exceeding that required for an officer for advancement to flag rank . . . that it is desirable to advance him the rank of Rear Admiral . . .'. The Queen was happy to approve the recommendation and Alfred, Duke of Edinburgh, achieved his great wish of reaching flag rank by his own efforts.

In November 1879 Alfred took up his new appointment as Admiral Superintendent of Naval Reserves, hoisting his flag aboard the 4394-ton corvette HMS *Penelope* at Harwich. The First Reserve, of which the *Penelope* was flagship, comprised the armour plated ships *Audacious*, *Belleisle*, *Hector*, *Hercules*, *Lord Warden*, *Resistance*, *Valiant* and *Warrior* and eight gunboats. The Duke brought to his appointment his professionalism and skills, working the ships up to a high standard of efficiency, each year taking the reserve ships to sea with the Channel Squadron. It was this more

*One of the duties that Prince Alfred carried out while Admiral
Superintendent of Naval Reserves was the opening of the new Eddystone
lighthouse in May 1882. He was accompanied by the young Battenberg
and the ceremony was attended by many US men-of-war. (National
Maritime Museum)*

prestigious squadron to which the Duke was subsequently appointed as C-in-C in December 1883 as Vice Admiral, a rank he
attained a year earlier. His flag was hoisted in the armour plated
Minotaur; when built some fifteen years previously she and her
sister ships *Agincourt* and *Northumberland* had the double distinction of being—at 400 feet—the largest single-screw warships ever
built and the most heavily armed vessels: they each carried four
9-inch MLR, twenty-four 7-inch MLR and eight 24-pounder
guns. Alfred's two years of command were spent chiefly in exercising his squadron and enhancing his reputation and skills in fleet
manoeuvres. The Duke had developed into a truly professional
sailor and this experience prepared him for one of the most glitter-

ing of naval appointments, that of C-in-C Mediterranean.

On 5 March 1886 Alfred arrived at Valetta and transferred to his flagship, the *Alexandra* with all the pomp and ceremony that accompanied a supreme commander arriving on his station.

HMS *Alexandra* was the same flagship that Alfred had known eight years earlier in the Dardenelles incident when he commanded the *Sultan*, and this latter ship was still in the fleet now under his command. The fleet comprised a variety of vessels, for the navy was still in transition and armaments were still influencing design: *Alexandra*, *Sultan* and *Superb* were broadside ships; *Temeraire* was a barbette ship; *Dreadnought* and *Agamemnon* were turret ships; *Neptune* and *Thunderer* were twin-screwed ironclads; there were armoured broadside corvettes *Orion* and *Carysfort*, the torpedo ram *Polyphemus*, sloops, gunboats, and torpedo boats. Alfred's was, in truth, a fleet in transition.

His three-year tenure of office was comparatively free of wars and hostilities apart from problems in the Balkans which called for a blockade of the Greek coasts; so Alfred was denied the chance to distinguish his career with daring exploits.

When an uneasy peace had been restored to the Balkans the Duke paid a ceremonial visit to the Sultan of Turkey, accompanied by his young nephew, Lieutenant the Prince George—later King George V—a serving officer aboard HMS *Thunderer*. Another member of the royal family serving in the fleet at this time was Prince Louis of Battenberg as commander of the *Dreadnought*. He, his wife Victoria and their five children had moved to Malta for the duration of his commission, where they were frequent visitors to the C-in-C's home in Valetta where Uncle Affie and Aunt Alice welcomed their spirited and lively company.

The years on the Mediterranean station were privileged and pleasurable for Alfred and they passed in tranquil, leisurely fashion, made doubly enjoyable because his duchess and the children were with him, living in the large and impressive residence of San Antonio. The sun shone brightly on Alfred during this commission in the course of which he was promoted to full Admiral, the first royal sailor to have achieved that rank on merit. But the commission ended and in April 1889 Alfred struck his flag as C-in-C and returned to Portsmouth in the *Alexandra* where she was paid off.

HMS Alexandra *is pictured here during the bombardment of the forts of Alexandria in 1882. (National Maritime Museum)*

Their Lordships at the Admiralty set the seal on this happy interlude in Alfred's life by commending him for 'the zealous and efficient manner in which he discharged on all occasions the many anxious and responsible duties devolving on him as Commander-in-Chief, Mediterranean'.

Alfred's next appointment—and his last active naval post—was as C-in-C Plymouth, an appointment which lasted almost three years—until June 1893. On relinquishing command Prince Alfred was promoted to Admiral of the Fleet and thus achieved the rare distinction of serving from cadet to the topmost rank in the navy, a career which spanned thirty-five years.

On 22 August 1893 he succeeded to the title of his late uncle—the Duke of Saxe-Coburg-Gotha—and thereafter saw a decline in his pleasures: in an age of heavy drinking he was regarded as a heavy drinker and it was probably alcohol which contributed to the cancer which later afflicted his throat. After adopting the new title it was then ruled that he could retain his naval rank but forgo the right to attend the House of Lords.

Prince Alfred, Duke of Edinburgh

In 1897 the aged Queen Victoria wished to mark her jubilee by a presentation to her Affie of a special baton—a rarely bestowed gift to an admiral of the fleet. 'On the occasion of her Jubilee,' the announcement declared, 'Queen Victoria was pleased to present to her dear son HRH The Duke of Saxe-Coburg and Gotha, Duke of Edinburgh, KG, a baton as Admiral of the Fleet.'

The aged Queen outlived her darling Affie, for on 30 July 1900, a year before her own death, Prince Alfred died of the cancer in his throat. His had been a fruitful life of service to his country, unlike the wasted years of some of his royal predecessors: he was truly a professional if taciturn royal admiral.

6
Prince Louis of Battenberg

ON QUEEN VICTORIA's thirty-fifth birthday, 24 May 1854, a son was born at Graz in Austria to Julie, Countess of Battenberg, wife of Prince Alexander of Hesse. The baby boy was christened Louis Alexander but he was to achieve naval renown in the Royal Navy as Admiral Prince Louis of Battenberg, and some would say that he was to achieve greater fame for fathering an even greater admiral —Earl Mountbatten of Burma.

The baby's father, Prince Alexander of the small Prussian State of Hesse, had eloped in 1851 with the Countess Julie von Hauke and committed the blunder of a morganatic marriage with her at Breslau. The courts of Europe ostracized the couple; Alexander's brother, the Grand Duke Louis III of Hesse, led the family disapproval; Queen Victoria even expressed her anger and dismay. It took a few years for the Grand Duke to relent and when he did so it was with magnanimity for he even searched about for a suitable name and rank for the couple. He settled on the name of a dreamy village on the banks of the River Eder in the north of Hesse, a pocket-sized principality of the one-time seat of a defunct knightly family. The village, in what is now west central Germany, was called Battenberg.

Julie was created Countess of Battenberg. Alexander, of course, retained the style of HRH the Prince Alexander, and some years later the Grand Duke raised Julie to the rank of Her Serene Highness and allowed the children of the marriage to be styled princes and princesses. Alexander took his family to the newly built Alexander Palace in Darmstadt—the winter residence—and to the Schloss Heilingenberg, ten miles to the south, the summer retreat. It was Heilingenberg that was to become the Battenberg family's

Schloss Heilingenberg, near Darmstadt, Prince Louis's beloved childhood home to which he was to return as a high-ranking officer in the British navy. (Broadlands Archives)

favourite home, basically a substantial farmhouse expensively enlarged by wings and towers until it could accommodate sixty guests or more. Entertainment of just about everyone who was anyone in the courts of Europe was on a regal scale with constant comings and goings to Heilingenberg.

It was against this elegant backdrop that the eight-year-old Prince Louis Battenberg began his settled home life, by which time he spoke fluent English, German, Russian and Italian, was less fluent in French, could draw skilfully, was tall for his age and notably handsome. He was described by his sister Marie as 'looking like a Velasquez when he was older, like a Raphael when he was young'.

Another Darmstadt resident was the English Princess Alice and her husband Ludwig. The Battenberg children were frequent visitors to their house and it was there that they met Prince Alfred in 1867, a ridiculously young twenty-three-year-old captain in the Royal Navy, who captivated them with his fascinating stories of the world's greatest navy. Prince Louis, now thirteen, expressed a genunine and sincere interest in the navy and on one occasion asked Alfred if it were possible for a foreign prince to serve in the Royal Navy. When Louis's parents learned of his wish they were appalled;

the military tradition in Hesse was strong and the Battenberg heir was destined for the army. Prince Louis secured an ally in Princess Alice, and he argued long with his parents before they yielded to his wish to serve in the Royal Navy.

Princess Alice persuaded her mother Queen Victoria to have the age limit for entry into the Royal Navy raised from fourteen to fourteen-and-a-half years, allowing Louis time to spend the summer and autumn of 1868 in cramming for the entrance examination for the Naval College at Portsmouth in December. A Mr Everett was despatched from Magdalen College, Oxford, as special tutor in algebra, Euclid, Latin and English composition. It was a long hot summer in Heilingenberg for Louis so the departure for England on 25 September came as a welcome interlude. Once in England he joined a school in Alverstoke, between Gosport and Portsmouth, where twenty other boys were cramming for the same entrance examination under the headmastership of Dr Burney, who assiduously kept Louis apart from the other boys. Dr Burney took Louis to a notary public in Gosport where the boy took an oath of allegiance to the Queen—noting with distaste that he was asked to kiss a very dirty bible. He also visited Uncle Affie's tailor for a full dress uniform fit to meet the Queen, and often dined with the C-in-C Portsmouth, Admiral Sir Thomas Pasley.

The examination took place on 14 December and Louis passed comfortably and jubilantly to emerge as Cadet His Serene Highness the Prince Louis of Battenberg RN in ample time for Christmas leave in Heilingenberg and with the exciting prospect of going to sea in the new year in the training ship *Bristol*. But unwelcome intervention by Princess Alice and Uncle Bertie (Edward, Prince of Wales) secured for the young cadet an appointment as ADC to the Prince of Wales for a Mediterranean cruise: splendour and majesty there would be aplenty, but naval instruction and training, which was what Louis's contemporaries were receiving aboard the *Bristol*, would be denied him.

The *Ariadne* was a ten-year-old frigate converted in Malta to a temporary royal yacht. She was lying in Trieste harbour where Louis joined her at the end of January 1869 a week before the Prince and Princess of Wales. Louis had to cope with the dichotomy of being the youngest and greenest midshipman in the gunroom, yet the most privileged in terms of dining with their royal highnesses and accompanying them on their trips ashore. Louis found it all incredibly difficult.

Alexandria was reached in a few days and there began the glittering Royal Nile Expedition. In Cairo the rich and powerful Khedive of Egypt greeted the royal party. In Suez, Ferdinand de Lesseps was presented to them. At Port Said the party embarked on the Khedive's yacht—'a wonder of the day'—for the passage back to Alexandria. The yacht was fitted out with elegance and splendour, regardless of cost. On leaving harbour and clearing the breakwater the ship gave two or three heavy rolls. Louis later described what happened:

> The whole of the heavy gilt chairs on one side slid away to leeward with their occupants along the parquet floor to the ship's side, while the candelabra and fruit dishes fell over with a great clatter. At the next roll the chairs on the other side slid away, leaving the bare table deserted. At the same time piles of plates which stood on the marble consoles along each wall crashed down in two avalanches; most of the lights also went out. Needless to say, the Khedive's servants were sprawling on the floor, mixed up with the guests, and the general wreckage. A few minutes later the ship was once more steady as a church . . .

The splendours of entertainment in Egypt were dwarfed by the magnificence of the Sultan of Turkey's banquets in the Palace Saleh Bazar. Thence, the royal party steamed to Sevastopol where Louis visited the famous Crimean battlefields and himself cantered and galloped into the Valley of Death like the six hundred.

In Greece the *Ariadne* anchored in the Piraeus and the Princess of Wales was specially delighted at entertaining her brother, the King of Greece, aboard for lunch. Entertainment ashore, again, was on a lavish scale. On the island of Corfu Louis met Queen Olga who was still nursing her new born boy, destined to become King Constantine, brother of Prince Andrew of Greece—the father of Prince Philip.

But these splendid days for Louis were to end at Brindisi where the Prince of Wales left the frigate and Cadet Louis, deprived of royal patronage, returned to the harsh privations of the gunroom on the seemingly endless passage to England; living in a friendless community, enduring the toughness of working aloft, Louis became increasingly depressed and disenchanted with life in the navy and pleaded for his release. But moderation prevailed and after a spell of leave at Heilingenberg with parents and friends Louis was content to resume his naval duties. His appointment in July 1869 was to HMS *Royal Alfred*, the flagship of the North American station, whose C-in-C was Vice Admiral G. Wellesley. The admiral and the entire crew, who included many of the familiar midshipmen's faces from the *Ariadne*, were to be shipped out to Halifax in the single-screw line-of-battleship *Revenge*, a two decker, which ran into heavy weather in the Atlantic crossing, a crossing marked by the exhilaration of working aloft in a gale, sighting icebergs and having the gunroom flooded.

The *Royal Alfred*, named after Alfred, the Duke of Edinburgh,

The Royal Alfred *which Prince Louis joined as a midshipman in 1869.*
(Imperial War Museum)

was completed in 1865 after an interrupted birth: she began life as a wooden two decker but before completion the French startled naval circles throughout Europe by building the world's first iron-clad and the Admiralty decided to transform the wooden ship by cladding her with 6-inch thick iron plating and the mounting of a heavy armament of 9-inch and 7-inch guns. When completed she could sail at 12 knots under a full spread of canvas or under steam-power from her 3000 horsepower engine.

The *Royal Alfred* commission in North American and West Indies waters was to last more than four-and-a-half years with the winter months spent in the Caribbean and the summer ones in northern waters. They were years of tedium, boredom and monot-ony, as sailors throughout history would assert that foreign com-missions usually are, punctuated by short bursts of interest. When winter approached the C-in-C closed down his shore-based resi-dence, embarked his family, house servants, horses and grooms, cattle, sheep and poultry, fodder and feed—lock stock and barrel—then disembarked the lot into the new residence at Admiralty House in Bermuda for the winter.

The British squadron spent a good deal of time cruising and visiting ports throughout the station with each visit marked by balls and dinners and ceremonies where the young Prince Louis was in demand. Once such visit was made by the C-in-C visiting Demerara in the frigate *Sirius* accompanied by Louis, in the course of which he witnessed a flogging, noting with observant detail that the second three dozen lashes were laid on by a left-handed boat-swain's mate. 'It was a gruesome sight,' Louis recorded. These years in the *Royal Alfred* were formative years for a young midship-man who was experiencing his first love affairs, notably with Isabel Macpherson over whom he wept inconsolably, and laying the foundations of lasting naval friendships.

In December 1873 the *Royal Alfred* was sent home to be paid off. Louis hurried impatiently to his beloved Heilingenberg, re-turning to England to cram for his sub-lieutenant's examinations, staying the while at the Royal Naval College, Greenwich. It was a time of intense court activity, with Alfred, the Duke of Edinburgh having just married Louis's Russian cousin, the Grand Duchess Marie, in St Petersburg, who on return to the English Court be-

Prince Louis was an accomplished artist. A number of his drawings, including this one showing the Prince of Wales boarding the Serapis *at Brindisi, were published in the* Illustrated London News. *The picture is signed with the artist's initials. (* Illustrated London News *)*

came engrossed in celebrations and festivities, which Louis, as Alfred's protégé, found it impossible to avoid. The hectic round of banquets and balls left no mark, fortunately, on Louis's examination results. For seamanship he not only passed out first, but was the best student ever; for gunnery he also came first and joint best student ever.

In 1875 Prince Louis was invited to join the all-male party to accompany the Prince of Wales for the Royal Tour of India, a tour conducted in a manner appropriate to the imperial majesty of the heir to the throne. Another young naval officer in the party was the hot-tempered Lieutenant Lord Charles Beresford, another favourite of the Prince of Wales. The departure of the royal train from an illuminated Charing Cross station to Brindisi was accompanied by a military band and bagpipes. In France the Prince lunched with the French President and attended the theatre with the Compte de Paris, which helped relieve the tedium of the long rail journey to Brindisi on the heel of Italy to board the *Serapis*. This vessel a converted Indian troopship, commanded by Captain the Hon. H. Carr Glyn, acted as the royal yacht. As sub-lieutenant of the gunroom Prince Louis suffered the cramped accommodation of his midshipmen although he managed to secure himself a small cabin, but as a favoured member of the royal party he was privileged to dine in the wardroom, attend the magnificent State visits, ceremonials and sporting events, the first of which occurred in Greece.

No official explanation has been revealed for Captain Glyn's extraordinary behaviour when the *Serapis* arrived in the Piraeus in the presence of the whole Greek Navy, important elements of the British Mediterranean Fleet and the Greek Royal Yacht *Amphitrite*, assembled to greet the Prince of Wales. The *Serapis* approached the anchorage at great speed, overshot her billet, overcompensated in going astern, lost two anchors, narrowly missed colliding with several ships in the crowded anchorage and collided with the *Amphitrite*, taking away her bowsprit.

A gentler approach was made when the *Serapis* and accompanying warships sailed up the Hoogly River to Calcutta where the squadron arrived on Christmas Eve; the Prince of Wales was presented with priceless jewels and the gift of a tiger, but the most breathtaking sight was at Benares where a city of tents had been set up with unmatched splendour. Louis's own tent was fully furnished with a double bedroom, bathroom, dressing-room, armchairs, writing table and a brick fireplace! Grooms stood by with a fine selection of Arab horses while servants were on duty to meet his every request. Louis wrote of the enormous divan with soft cushions and, in common with other members of the royal party, a native girl in transparent white garments provided for his pleasure.

The princes, maharajahs and potentates vied with each other in the lavishness of their hospitality. Hunting figured high in the sporting lists. At Agra, Louis Battenberg, out for boar, took a spill and broke a collar bone. In Nepal, the Prime Minister, Sir Jung Bahardur, treated the royal visitors to a week of hunting, with one thousand elephants and 10,000 attendant troops; on his first day the Prince of Wales bagged six tigers from his rocking howdah.

While Louis was in India the Duke of Edinburgh invited him to join the battleship *Sultan*, then in the Mediterranean.

To serve aboard a battleship in the finest fleet in the world was exciting and Louis hurried on the long journey to Naples where the Russian cruiser *Svetlana* lay at anchor with cousin Alexei aboard, thence to Messina, to Malta, and finally by a run-down gunboat to the Dardenelles where HMS *Sultan* was located in Belsika Bay. Louis was suprised by the run-down state of the fleet and by contrast Uncle Alfie's curious habit of wearing all orders and decorations at the drop of a hat. He indulged this habit on the ship's visit to the Crimea where the Emperor and numerous other members of the Russian royal family were entertained in splendour, and in the Piraeus where the Greek royal family visited Alfred, accompanied as usual by Louis.

On another cruise, 'PL' as Louis was known to his friends and messmates, accompanied Alfred and his family as a glorified seagoing general factotum and chamberlain, to Nice where they spent a few days with the Prince of Wales. During a visit to the new Casino at Monte Carlo for an evening of *rouge et noir*, Louis put an old gold *louis* on red and let it ride nine times. He had to fashion a makeshift bag from a towel to carry his winnings to the bank.

Louis quickly grew to dislike the naval equerry status which his appointment seemed to have reached, denying him the involvement in ships' and squadrons' duties normally associated with a young naval officer's career.

The state of the fleet, in decline under the command of the deaf, elderly Admiral the Hon. Sir James Drummond, revived when Admiral Phipps-Hornby joined the station as C-in-C, and instigated drills, exercises and evolutions which soon began to have their effect both on morale and efficiency. But it was the social life which dominated the Mediterranean scene and Louis immersed himself in the sporting activities which abounded, including horse racing and polo in Malta, and hunting and shooting at other ports of call. So important was sport to the officers that a pack of hunting beagles was brought to the Mediterranean at considerable expense and drafted to HMS *Agincourt*. Collapsible kennels and stables were constructed aboard the ship, the beagles and ponies quartered below decks, and with the onset of winter the fleet steamed for

Belsika Bay where the kennels would be set up ashore and a proper hunt established with sailors trained as huntsmen and whips. They were incredible days, divorced from the harsh realities of seafaring, until the Russo-Turkish war and the Constantinople campaign and the spy scandal already related, the result of which was a near mutinous Louis, smarting under the injustice of virtually being dismissed his ship, returned to Heilingenberg.

Louis's father supported the view that the Battenberg family name had been insulted by Queen Victoria and it was only on receipt of a grudging and qualified apology via Princess Alice that Louis agreed not to resign his commission and at the invitation of the Prince of Wales journeyed to London where any lingering doubts about the British royal family's feelings toward him were dispelled. The Prince of Wales entertained him royally at Marlborough House, the First Lord (W. H. Smith of bookstore fame) invited him to the Admiralty and reassured him about his future while the Queen gave her gracious seal of approval by inviting the young officer to lunch. Louis was won over by all this attention and any vestige of doubt was finally dispelled in the following year when the Queen invited both Louis and Sandro to Balmoral. 'Both Sandro and Louis are so amiable, intelligent and nice, so well brought up,' the Queen wrote in her journal.

1880 was a year marked by two events of drama in Louis's life, the first of which was a narrow escape from death when a bomb of of enormous destructive power exploded in a fifth assassination attempt on the life of the Tsar in the Winter Palace at St Petersburg. The Tsar, Louis, Sandro and the grand dukes all escaped with their lives and only suffered minor injuries.

The second incident had a more creative and lasting effect than the bomb attack. In March of 1880 he met and fell passionately in love with one of the most beautiful women in London society, a lady who was also—more dangerously—the mistress of the Prince of Wales: the actress Lillie Langtry. They must have made a well-matched couple; she, the famed Jersey Lily, one of the world's beauties and he, one of Europe's most handsome and elegant princes. So clandestine and discreet was their lovemaking that few people learned of their affair which was sincere and passionate. It ended abruptly with Lillie's unexpected pregnancy. She behaved

Lillie Langtry, the mistress of the Prince of Wales, with whom Prince Louis fell passionately in love. (Victoria and Albert Museum)

with amazing compliance in avoiding scandal and in preserving the good name of the Battenbergs: a courier was sent from Darmstadt and arranged a financial settlement, the affair was hushed up and, significantly, the Admiralty immediately gave Louis an appointment to the *Inconstant* which was to embark on a round-the-world tour. When the child was born—a daughter named Jeanne-Marie—the sailor father was far away.

The *Inconstant* was an iron frigate of 5800 tons, splendid to look at and fast under either canvas or steam; she wore the flag of Rear Admiral the Earl of Clanwilliam as Commander of the Detached or Flying Squadron. He was tall, hawk-nosed and dark-bearded and suffered pain from a severe bullet wound in the arm suffered at Canton. This squadron comprised four screw corvettes, the *Carysfort, Cleopatra, Tourmaline,* and *Bacchante,* led by the *Inconstant.* The *Bacchante* was commanded by Captain Lord Charles Scott, the younger brother of the Duke of Buccleuch, who was also charged with the responsibility of the Prince of Wales's two sons, the cadets Prince Eddy and Prince George, just embarking on a naval career.

Lieutenant Louis Battenberg joined the flagship along with Percy Scott, another young lieutenant who was to have a profound influence upon the strategy, tactics and technology of gunnery in the Royal Navy, and together they set off on 16 October 1880 for a cruise that was to last two years and a feature of which was to be the demonstration of the Royal Navy's determination to retain sails in preference to steam.

The squadron reached the wide estuary of the River Plate and sailed into Montevideo before Christmas and it was here that a remarkable incident occurred. The British Minister to Uruguay, the Hon. Edward T. Monson, attended a garden party at El Prado in Montevideo, organized in honour of the Princes and the British squadron and attended by officers from visiting ships from America, Brazil and Spain. The Minister was just about to propose marriage to his partner for the evening ball when he was handed a telegram. He stuffed it in his pocket and in the euphoria of having his proposal accepted promptly forgot it until the squadron had sailed a few days later and his valet brought it to his attention. Monson was horrified to read the instructions ordering the squadron to proceed forthwith to Simon's Bay to land guns and a thousand men to put down a rebellion in South Africa. Monson despatched a gunboat with all haste to recall the south-bound squadron but it was at the Falkland Islands before the gunboat finally overhauled

Prince Louis fell in love with Lillie Langtry as a young man of twenty-six. Still a superbly handsome man we see him here— Captain Prince Louis of Battenberg—at the age of forty. (Imperial War Museum)

Clanwillian who was already preparing to round Cape Horn. The squadron set off for Simon's Bay and arrived there twenty-two days later on 17 February.

It was while Louis was in South Africa that he learned of the final murderous success of the Russian Nihilists in an explosive assassination of his Uncle Alexander, Tsar Alexander II, in a carriage in St Petersburg.

Meanwhile, in South Africa, the plans for the Flying Squadron were changed and the ships proceeded to Australia and thence to Japan. One month out of Simon's Bay while in the Roaring Forties, the squadron ran into fierce storms with mountainous seas crashing astern in which the ships rolled frighteningly. When the storm abated a safe landfall was made at Albany in Western Australia.

The battered ships sailed for Melbourne where repairs were effected and the opportunity was taken to transfer the Princes to the *Inconstant*. Louis's future cousins by marriage came to know him well during the ensuing months in the long voyage across the Pacific to China and Japan, visiting islands and ports throughout South-East Asia, including a visit to the King of Fiji. A highlight of the Pacific experience was a meeting with the Mikado and his Empress in Tokyo but perhaps the most important feature of the voyage was the friendship that developed between Louis and the future King George V which was to endure for the rest of their lives.

Louis left Tokyo—with the addition of a tattooed dragon on his left arm—on the homeward passage visiting Kobe, Singapore

Prince Louis captures the mood of a Sunday afternoon at sea aboard HMS Inconstant *in 1882. (Broadlands Archives)*

(where his son was to accept the Japanese surrender sixty-five years later), Colombo, Aden and Gibraltar, where on 2 July 1882 a message was received ordering *Inconstant* to proceed to Egypt to help put down an insurrection. The Sultan of Turkey had forced out of office the Khedive of Egypt and the army under a ruthless Brigadier Arabi Pasha had seized control in a bloody coup.

On the day that the *Inconstant* arrived at Malta an ultimatum to Arabi Pasha expired and the naval bombardment of the Alexandria forts and cannons began under the watchful eyes of the C-in-C himself, Admiral Sir Frederick Seymour. He witnessed a fearless attack by Lord Charles Beresford who distinguished himself by steaming his ship, the *Condor*, to within point-blank range of the Egyptian guns. At the end of the day the guns had surrendered.

Louis was disconsolate at arriving too late for the naval bombardment but was mollified at the prospect of action ashore when armed parties of sailors were sent to protect the town against Arabi's army of 20,000 soldiers. Louis led a party of blue-jackets across the rubble of Alexandria with a battery of six Gatling machine guns which fired a stream of bullets at the cranking of a handle. Percy Scott exercised his special gunnery expertise by mounting a battery of guns ashore and exchanging salvoes with Arabi's guns. The prize for enterprise, if nothing else, went to Captain 'Jacky' Fisher of the *Inflexible*, accompanied by Lord Charles Beresford, who were later to become arch enemies, for their equipping a train as an armoured train and thundering off into the outlying desert. These adventures came to an end when General Wolseley roundly defeated Arabi's army at Tel-el-Kebir, and a month later—on 16 October—the *Inconstant* was at Spithead and Louis was soon enjoying the autumn balls and parties as guest of the Prince of Wales at Marlborough House.

Once back at Darmstadt Louis strengthened his ties with England by courting Queen Victoria's grand-daughter, the daughter of Princess Alice and the Grand Duke Louis IV of Hesse, the beautiful teenager, Princess Victoria. Louis made the announcement to Prince George, his shipmate, in a letter in the spring of 1883 from his beloved Heilingenberg: 'My dearest Georgie, I have a great piece of news to tell you. Our mutual cousin Victoria has promised to be my wife! I can't tell you how happy I am. She is such a lovely

103

darling girl, as you know, and I am nearly off my chump altogether with feeling so jolly.' He signed himself: 'Ever your affectionate old shipmate, Louis.'

The marriage—on 30 April 1884—was a sumptuous event, the wedding of the decade at the Grand Ducal Palace, with fluttering bunting and flags giving an air of festival to Darmstadt while Schloss Heilingenberg offered hospitality to the courts of Europe. Queen Victoria headed the long list of royalty; the Prince of Wales and Princess Alexandra also represented Great Britain; also attending were grand dukes and duchesses, princes and princesses; Romanoffs, Habsburgs, Badens, Hohenzollerns, Würtemburgs, Coburgs, Bourbons, Germans, British, Russians and the Scandinavian Oscars and Christians—it was a glittering and royal occasion with Louis in full-dress naval lieutenant's uniform wearing the Grand Cross of the Order of the Bath and the Star of the Hessian Order of Louis and Chain. It was to be a joyous and lasting marriage.

Louis Battenberg's naval career now entered a period of doldrums, which should have been relieved by his promotion to Commander on 30 August 1885 but the gilt was knocked off the gingerbread because no suitable appointment could be found for him and he was put on to half pay for very close to two years. Things improved when his next appointment came through as commander aboard the 10,820-tons battleship *Dreadnought*, pride of the Royal Navy with the thickest armour plating of any battleship. The appointment aroused controversy in the House of Commons. 'Is it true . . . that Prince Louis of Battenberg has been appointed to the command of HMS *Dreadnought* over the heads of 30 or 40 officers having superior qualifications?' The Irish questioner had confused the role of 'commander' with 'in command' but the accusation of privilege was made. It was the most serious public attack upon Louis thus far and it wounded him. He had shrugged off the barbs of years which had cut and irritated him and the hostility of fellow officers and politicians because of his German origins and princely patronage.

Louis travelled to join his battleship in Malta in company with Prince George, now a lieutenant and about to take up an appointment in Uncle Affie's flagship, *Alexandra*. Louis immersed himself in his new duties. Mark Kerr, a naval colleague and friend, the

C-in-C's flag lieutenant, later quoted a letter from Louis graphically describing coaling ship from a collier alongside:

> From Saturday, 4.30 a.m. until Monday forenoon I was in my clothes having my meals almost always standing, and only lying down on the deck, all dirty and greasy, for an hour's sleep at a time. It was very hard on the men, who worked incessantly, two halves relieving each other every two hours night and day and, having to work all through Sunday, they required a good deal of humouring. The heat was intense and with a burning sun.
>
> On the third day I was so worn out that I could hardly drag myself along. We hoisted in close on 1,000 bags, which had to be filled, then hoisted in, emptied and sent back for re-filling. I wonder what a Lieutenant-Colonel of the British Army would say if he was expected to do that in time of peace as a matter of ordinary routine?

The next few years were spent by Louis in uneventful cruising throughout the Mediterranean with interesting social life ashore in Malta which almost dominated everything else. Princess Victoria and her daughter, Alice, joined Louis in Malta and she soon acclimatized herself to the social rounds and spent much time with Prince Alfred and his Duchess Marie in their official residence of San Antonio where they ruled supreme with dinner parties and balls of majestic splendour. Hunting, shooting and fishing parties vied with picnics, polo and gymkhanas in a never-ending series and great opera companies visited the island to perform in the magnificent opera house. These were tranquil days enlivened by visits from relatives and friends from the royal courts of Britain, Germany and Russia—including a visit by Captain Alfred von Tirpitz, creator of the German battlefleet, the High Seas Fleet, that was to clash with the Royal Navy at Jutland.

3 October 1889 was a red-letter day for Commander Prince Louis of Battenberg's naval career—that rare day of appointment 'in command'. His command, the *Scout*, was an undistinguished vessel, a twin screwed torpedo boat built in 1885, displacing 1580 tons and carrying an armament of four 5-inch guns and seven torpedo tubes. She was manned by 145 officers and men. Commander Battenberg

applied all his considerable energies and enthusiasm to make the *Scout* a smart and disciplined ship. The ship saw some service in the Red Sea but during the winter of 1891-2 much time was spent in port and Louis devoted his inventive mind to the designing of an ingenious navigating instrument which became widely adopted throughout the Royal Navy. Princess Victoria much enjoyed relating the story of a Russian naval captain trying to persuade Tsar Nicholas II to adopt the Course Indicator: she told Nicholas that the correct name was the Battenberg Course Indicator whereupon the Tsar told the captain proudly, 'It may interest you to know that my brother-in-law invented this instrument' at which the captain burst out laughing thinking it a fine joke.

Louis's naval career followed a reasonably normal pattern: promotion to captain came with seniority and not patronage; appointment to the handsome cruiser HMS *Cambrian* was the reward of effort and leadership and in spite of rather than because of his associations with the Russian and British royal families; the Queen and the Prince of Wales, in particular, offered Louis favours which he found embarrassing; both had tried hard to persuade him to accept command of the royal yacht, for they both had a great affection for Louis, Victoria and their children.

The *Cambrian* was a brand new second-class cruiser of 4360 tons, mounting 6-inch guns and capable of 20 knots. She was a small ship, but Louis set out to make her the crack ship of the Mediterranean Fleet and just how successful he was is testified by his successor who described the ship as 'the smartest, most efficient and happiest ship that I have ever seen . . . I fear there is nothing I can add to the ship, as she has every record and cup on the station except the Veteran Officers' Race . . .'

It was predictable that a more important command should follow and in due course Louis was offered the battleship *Majestic*, flagship of the Channel Fleet. It was a wrench for the family to leave Malta and the Mediterranean which they had come to know and love so much but the compensations of even a modest home in London with ready access to the elegance of Buckingham Palace and the ageing Queen's court attracted the Battenbergs.

In June 1899 Prince Louis, now a forty-five-year-old captain and destined for even higher command, was given a shore appointment at the Admiralty as Assistant Director of Naval Intelligence and within a short time was being described as 'perhaps one of the two best officers in the whole British Navy' by his old senior officer, now Vice Admiral Sir John Fisher.

In the autumn of 1901 Louis took the battleship *Implacable* to the Mediterranean where Fisher was the C-in-C and from this date Fisher took Louis into his confidence; and Louis, repaying the compliment, declared himself a firm believer in the genius of Fisher, a view which he held at least until the Home Fleet controversy of 1906.

The *Implacable* commission in the Mediterranean was marked by two special features, each contributing substantially to Louis's professional standing. The first came about quite fortuitously when Rear Admiral Burgess Watson was taken ill and Captain Prince Louis of Battenberg took command of 'X' Fleet in an exercise to test a new theory about the close blockade of an enemy port. The Greek port of Argostoli containing 'X' Fleet was blockaded by 'A' and 'B' Fleets commanded respectively by Admiral Sir Compton Domville and Vice Admiral Sir Arthur 'Tug' Wilson, commanding between them 12 battleships, 16 cruisers and 14 destroyers. Louis's fleet comprised 8 battleships, 6 cruisers and 7 destroyers, and the purpose of the exercise was 'to ascertain what risks are involved in keeping such a close watch on a fleet in a defended port as to ensure bringing it to action if it issues therefrom.'

Louis's fleet 'issued therefrom' employing skills in fleet-handling, deception, camouflage, wireless telegraphy and seamanship of such a high order that his fleet escaped practically unscathed from a much superior blockading force, reaching Sardinia hours ahead of its red-faced pursuers. It was a spectacular achievement which aroused much embarrassment and made a lasting impression, resulting in the establishment of *distant* blockade as the means of containing an enemy force—such as was to be employed by the Grand Fleet at Scapa in blockading the German High Seas Fleet.

The second important feature of Louis's term in the Mediterranean was the exchange of critical memoranda between himself and Fisher. Louis's exchanges were lengthy, profound and numerous and they related specially to administrative aspects of the navy.

One of these so captured Fisher's imagination that he promptly wrote to Rear Admiral Lord Charles Beresford:

> What we want is *an additional naval member of the Board of Admiralty absolutely dissociated from all administrative and executive work and solely concerned in the* 'PREPARATION OF THE FLEET FOR WAR!' Battenberg has invented a magnificent name for him— 'THE WAR LORD' but as it is his copyright, you must get his permission to use it . . .*

Fisher's confidence in Louis was further evidenced in 1902, a year after the *Implacable* appointment, when Fisher became Second Sea Lord and he recalled Louis to the Admiralty as Director of Naval Intelligence. It was a reforming and innovating zeal with which Louis tackled the naval problems of the day and in which he was encouraged by both Fisher and his friend Bertie, now King Edward VII. It was a period of intense and satisfying activity, during which Louis displayed broad vision in almost everything he undertook, including the creation of the Imperial Defence College. It is true to say that at the turn of the century the Royal Navy needed the reforming drive of Battenberg and the explosive, arrogant dogma of Fisher whose declared creed for war he also applied to his high command peacetime duties: 'Ruthless! Relentless! Remorseless!'—his famous Three Rs. By the time Fisher was appointed First Sea Lord—on Trafalgar Day 1904—he and Louis had formed a strong working partnership cemented by the common aim to strengthen the navy and minimize what they discerned as the growing threat of German sea power—in which fleet incidentally, Louis's brother-in-law Prince Henry enjoyed high command.

Inevitably, reformers attract opponents and enemies: Fisher, in particular, generated violent reactions, notably from the 'syndicate of discontent' led by the hero of the bombardment of Alexandria, the eccentric Lord Charles Beresford; these same malcontents turned their antagonism on Prince Louis when he was promoted

---

* *Fear God and Dread Nought :* The Correspondence of Admiral of the Fleet Lord Fisher of Kilverstone, Selected and Edited by Arthur J. Marder, Vol.I, p.232, Jonathan Cape, 1952.

Rear Admiral in 1904 which drew forth a comment from the King who expressed anxiety for the possible harm being done to Louis. 'I have never known more malignant rancour and jealousy', Fisher wrote, 'as manifested by Lord Charles Beresford and Hedworth Lambton as against Prince Louis.' Louis, understandably, was bitter: 'Beresford and Lambton', he wrote, 'and all that tribe gave out . . . that I was a damned German who had no business in the British Navy . . . a drop of poison in my cup of happiness of a lifetime devoted truly and wholly to our great service . . .'

The redoubtable Lord Fisher commemorated in this vivid portrait by Augustus John. (Leicester Art Gallery)

Beresford's vindictiveness reached a peak when he wrote a letter to all the London newspapers stating that Louis's name should be removed from the Navy List because of his German birth. No paper carried the letter but the seeds of doubt were being sown that would be reaped many years later. Louis escaped from these harsh political manoeuvrings in Whitehall and took up his appointment as Rear Admiral Commanding the Second Cruiser Squadron— which must have seemed like a breath of fresh air—hoisting his flag in HMS *Drake*, flagship of a squadron of six modern armoured cruisers in February 1905. The four-funnelled *Drake* displaced 14,100 tons and mounted two 9-inch and sixteen 6-inch guns. The rest of the squadron were county-class ships of 9800 tons each carrying fourteen 6-inch guns: *Essex, Cornwall, Berwick, Cumberland* and *Bedford*.

Before the end of the year Louis was to entertain a host of VIPs aboard his cruiser and climaxed the year by making an official visit to the USA and meeting President Theodore 'Teddy' Roosevelt at the White House. In preparation for the visit the *Drake* squadron went to the Mediterranean to work up to a peak of efficiency and while there the cruiser was visited by the Kaiser, Wilhelm II, who held the honorary rank of Admiral of the Fleet in the Royal Navy, and Louis pleased him enormously by breaking the Union flag at the masthead as the Kaiser came aboard. The King and Queen of Greece were entertained aboard as were the King and Queen of Portugal; in Greece Louis saw his daughter Princess Alice and her husband Prince Andrew, the future father of Prince Philip.

In August the crack squadron sailed west for the Americas where the Dominion of Canada was visited first and Louis and the crews of his ships first tasted the hospitality that was to be lavished on them in the following weeks both in Canada and the USA. For Louis it was to be an unforgettable experience that he was to cherish the rest of his life, despite the exhausting receptions, luncheons and dinners, each with the obligatory speech. His love of America was inherited in full measure by his son, Dickie Mountbatten. The visit to Annapolis, 'home' of the US Navy in Maryland, provided the opportunity to show off the squadron's seamanship, but Washington provided the diplomatic highlight—the meeting with Teddy Roosevelt and a dinner reception at the White House.

The technical highpoint of the visit came in New York where the ships of the British squadron were to anchor two cables apart only two cables from the US Fleet commanded by Rear Admiral Robley ('Fighting Bob') Evans. The eyes of America would be on the British ships, but more importantly they would be under the critical scrutiny of the US Navy. Louis resolved to make a spectacular arrival. The Hudson River was congested with beflagged small boats, yachts, steamers and ferries; multitudes thronged the banks cheering and waving as the six cruisers steamed against the ebbing tide in line ahead at 18 knots, black smoke streaming aft. They made a splendid sight. Abreast of Government Island they broke the Stars and Stripes at the main and fired a 21-gun salute. Tragedy was narrowly averted when a ferryboat crammed with seven hundred passengers—incredibly—passed through the squadron and a collision seemed inevitable. Disaster was averted by yards only, by the *Cornwall*'s evasive action. The cruisers sped to their anchorage till they came on to their bearings then went full astern and let go anchors: all six commanding officers waited anxiously for their ships to lose way and to complete the evolution with perfection. Nothing like it had been seen before. With equal dexterity dressing flags

Rear Admiral Robley ('Fighting Bob') Evans is pictured here greeting Prince Louis during his visit to the US Naval Academy, Annapolis. (Broadlands Archives)

were run up, standards broken at the masts and salutes fired. It was a masterly piece of showmanship.

A new round of luncheons, dinners and receptions followed,

every day for eleven days, in the course of which Louis and his staff attended a lunch in Chinatown. Louis's waiter was someone who later earned fame for his song composing—Irving Berlin—who earned himself a paragraph in the next morning's paper, the first time his name appeared in print. The visit to New York ended with a reception and ball for 1200 aboard HMS *Drake*, moored alongside the Cunard Line pier, a prized social event described as 'one of the most notable affairs ever held in New York'.

As if to clear his mind of weeks of socializing Louis ordered his six cruisers on leaving New York to race across the Atlantic to Gibraltar, a distance of 3327 miles. The *Drake* won in seven days seven hours—only a few minutes ahead of the *Berwick*—at an average speed of 18.5 knots. It was an incredible performance. On arrival back home in England Louis reported to the King and to Fisher before setting off for Christmas with the family at Heilingenberg.

HMS *Drake* achieved a supremacy over all other ships of the navy at target practice in December 1906. At a range of four miles 133 rounds were fired; 105 registered hits: it was a spectacular display of gunnery. When President Roosevelt learnt of these results he despatched his own plenipotentiary, Commander (later Admiral) Sims, to see how they had been obtained. Louis's arrogant, combative determination to be first and best in all he undertook had won the day yet again.

In February 1907 he was promoted acting Vice Admiral, Second-in-Command of the Mediterranean Fleet in the 15,000-ton battleship HMS *Venerable*; and nineteen months later he was appointed C-in-C of the Atlantic Fleet with his flag in the battleship, *Prince of Wales*.

These were days of reformation in the Royal Navy, days of discussion, dissension and discontent. The 'demonic' Admiral Fisher, First Sea Lord since 1904, a post he was to hold for six years, was a radical with far-reaching plans; he was the architect of Admiral Jellicoe's fleet of World War I, and an organizational genius who administered with passion, used memoranda as blunt instruments, and wrote them in CAPITALS. His years of office were studded with personality clashes, with struggles for power and controversies about many of his provocative ideas and methods. Even Louis clashed on more than one occasion with Fisher and their earlier alliance was soured. Louis tried to cope with an increasing anti-German sentiment being levelled against him. They were hard times. But in 1911 when relations with Germany were becoming increasingly strained Louis achieved one of his major aims, an Admiralty appointment as Second Sea Lord.

1911 was the year of a coronation: Louis's friend King Edward had gone; his cousin King George V had inherited an uneasy British crown; the irascible Fisher regime had ended and Germany was emerging as a naval menace; the rumblings of war could be discerned distantly. 'Every German vessel launched,' declared the Kaiser haughtily, 'is a guarantee for peace on earth. Every new warship makes it impossible for our enemies to attack us.' His ill-found confidence was to be disproved just three years later and it was the Kaiser's own cousin, Louis Battenberg, who contributed much to preparedness of the Royal Navy for the approaching clash of fleets. In 1912 amid much political uproar Louis was awarded the highest professional appointment in the navy by the young, ebullient First Lord, Winston Churchill, who later wrote of Louis:

> He had a far wider knowledge of war by land and sea and of the Continent of Europe than most of the other admirals I have known. He was deeply versed in every detail, practical and theoretical, of the British Naval Service . . . He was a thoroughly trained and accomplished staff officer, with the gift of clear and lucid statement.

The appointment revived the antagonisms of Lord Charles Beresford and his clique and although Churchill's eloquence and stubbornness won the day, resentment and bitterness lingered.

As First Sea Lord Louis experienced a partnership of twenty-three months with his dynamic and brilliant political chief whose tactlessness was to cause endless rows and was to test time and again the patience and good sense of Louis. One such minor crisis left some officers, according to Arthur Marder, in a state of 'choking wrath'. Stephen Roskill described another crisis as 'a cataclysmic row'. A lieutenant improperly told Churchill that his captain's decision regarding the use by the Naval Air Service of some land on the Medway was wrong. Churchill sent for the captain—G. W. Vivian—and challenged him. Vivian was enraged, complained to the C-in-C The Nore, Admiral Sir Richard Poore, who passed it on to the Second Sea Lord, Admiral Sir John Jellicoe. Churchill got to hear of this and his anger and subsequent ordering of the GPO to intercept and return some correspondence from Jellicoe to him, and his stated intention to order Poore to haul down his flag aroused ferocious indignation at the Admiralty. Jellicoe threatened to resign and the Third and Fourth Sea Lords told Louis that they, too, would join Jellicoe. Louis acted as intermediary for several days with comings and goings between his fellow Sea Lords and Churchill in an effort to resolve what Marder called Churchill's 'flagrant interference with the discipline of the fleet'. The matter was finally resolved by apologies all round and a chastened Churchill was only too anxious to avoid a mass resignation of the Board which would have precipitated his own downfall.

The near two years working with Churchill involved Louis in every major decision associated with the navy: he continued his deep interest which started when he was Second Sea Lord in the setting up of a Naval Air Service; the fleet was strengthened enormously in nearly every category of ship; he saw the introduction of the giant 15-inch gun into the fleet, of oil-fired boilers and, above all, by a cruel twist of fate, he supervised the strategy of planning a naval war with Germany, his land of birth.

In 1914 when the summer days of July brought the rumblings of war to a head the British Fleet was already mobilized and it was Louis's action as First Sea Lord, when Churchill was absent at the seaside on 16 July, in cancelling the demobilization of the fleet that was possibly the greatest decision of his career. A young midshipman—Prince Albert—later King George VI—aboard the dreadnought HMS *Collingwood* recorded: 'We left Portland . . . starting war routine at 1 p.m. After dinner we went to night defence stations, all ready for a destroyer attack and passed the Straits of Dover at midnight.' A few days later, the navy was ready for battle when needed.

But already the discontent with Louis's German ancestors was being voiced again in clubs, in letters to editors and even in the streets. Even his long-term friend, Fisher, now a still vigorous

*Prince Louis pictured with his family five years before his resignation.
The future Lord Mountbatten of Burma is half seated on his father's
knee. His elder brother, Georgie, is dressed as a midshipman. Princess
Louise later married King Gustav VI of Sweden. Her elder sister,
Princess Alice, who is absent from this picture, was already married to
Prince Andrew of Greece. (Broadlands Archives)*

seventy-four and anticipating his recall to his old office, began to
round on Louis; the opposition mounted and gathered momentum
like an Atlantic wave till it broke at the end of October and Louis
with uncomplaining dignity wrote to Winston Churchill:

> I have lately been driven to the painful conclusion that at this
> juncture my birth and parentage have the effect of impairing in
> some respects my usefulness on the Board of Admiralty. In these
> circumstances I feel it my duty, as a loyal subject of His Majesty,
> to resign the office of First Sea Lord, hoping thereby to facilitate
> the task of the administration of the great Service to which I have
> devoted my life, and to ease the burden laid on the Minister.

The blow of parting was ameliorated partly by the sympathy and warm friendship of Louis's colleagues at the Admiralty. His cousin, King George, admitted him a member of the Privy Council and Prince Louis retired with his family to the Isle of Wight just a few miles from the training college at Osborne where young Dickie was a cadet.

In 1917 even the royal family itself changed the family name to Windsor and in the same year the Battenbergs became Mountbattens and Louis himself, no longer His Serene Highness, was created 1st Marquess of Milford Haven, Earl of Medina and Viscount Alderney. In the following year Louis's family learned of the mass murder of their Russian relatives, Tsar Nicholas II, the Empress Alexandra, their four daughters and the young Tsarevitch, Alexis.

Louis was formally promoted to Admiral of the Fleet in 1921 but he only enjoyed this rank for a few weeks for on 11 September 1921 he died peacefully, at the age of sixty-seven.

7
King George V

PRINCE GEORGE was born at his parents' home, Marlborough House in London at 1.30 a.m. on the morning of 3 June 1865. He was the second son of the Prince of Wales (later King Edward VII) and Princess Alexandra, and grandson of the great Queen Victoria. He died over seventy years later on 20 January 1936 and he thus witnessed Britain reach the pinnacle of her imperial might in the Victorian era, and in the last two decades of his reign he lived through the years of Britain's imperial decline. This is not to say that he was a bad King or that he was responsible for this decline: indeed he is remembered with affection and is best described in the true old-fashioned phrase: 'a good King'.

George's life began with a squabble—about his names. Queen Victoria disliked *George*, preferring 'a fine old name' but she gave grudging approval to the second choice, Frederick. 'Of course,' she wrote imperiously to the Prince of Wales, 'you will add *Albert* at the end . . .' In the event, the baby was christened George Frederick Ernest Albert but in the family he was known as Georgie. His elder brother, Prince Albert Victor, known affectionately as Eddy, was to figure large in George's life, but the greatest influence upon the young prince was to be his mother, whom he addressed affectionately in letters as 'Darling Mother-dear'. From her he acquired the habit of reading a passage from the bible every day. His relationship with his father by contrast was tempered at first by awe and the fear of arousing his father's displeasure, but it later developed into a relationship of mutual confidence which was to last all of the Prince of Wales's life.

Most of George's childhood was spent at Sandringham and he developed a love of the house which was to last him all his life and, indeed, it was to be his last resting place as the dying King. The second great love of his life was the Royal Navy.

When the heir to the throne, Eddy, was seven and George nearly six, a tutor was employed for their full-time education. The Reverend John Neale Dalton, a thirty-two-year-old Cambridge don, became a devoted tutor for fourteen years and was a faithful friend of George's till he died at the age of ninety. Mr Dalton was a demanding taskmaster who kept the Princes to a rigid timetable with lessons starting before breakfast, with afternoons devoted to sports or riding and evenings ending with English, music and preparation, before bed at eight; it was a merciless régime. French lessons were under the tutelage of a Frenchman and drawing taught by an art master. When in London, army instructors taught the boys gymnastics, fencing and advanced riding skills at the Knightsbridge Barracks. At Sandringham George was taught to shoot at an early age and developed a love for the sport that lasted throughout his life.

Being the second son it had always been intended that George should enter the navy as a career: perhaps his father had been influenced by his brother, Alfred, the Duke of Edinburgh, who had not only escaped the palace schoolrooms but had patently enjoyed a naval education and upbringing.

In 1877, at the age of twelve it was time for George to enter the training ship *Britannia*, but complications arose over Eddy. The Queen wished the boy to go to Wellington School but Dalton had strong views on the matter and presented them persuasively. Eddy, he recommended, should accompany his brother George into the navy because Prince Albert Victor, Dalton wrote to the Queen, needed the stimulus of Prince George's company to induce him to work at all. Eddy, it seemed, was not very bright unless prodded into learning, and Dalton's persuasions prevailed. George passed his entry examination in June 1877 and joined the *Britannia* three months later accompanied by Eddy and Mr Dalton.

Ahead were two years of hard conditions for the Princes whose sole privilege was a cabin they shared—with Mr Dalton to watch over them. Otherwise, they suffered the uncongenial conditions, the rough canvas hammocks, the cold comfort of classrooms, and the harsh disciplines experienced by the other two hundred cadets. Their princely titles earned them no special favours. Indeed, Prince

George assured his librarian forty years later:

> It never did me any good to be a prince . . . far from making any allowances . . . the other boys made a point of taking it out on us on the grounds they'd never be able to do so later on. There was a lot of fighting among the cadets and the rule was that if challenged you had to accept. So they used to make me go up and challenge the bigger boys— I was awfully small then—and I'd get a hiding time and again . . .*

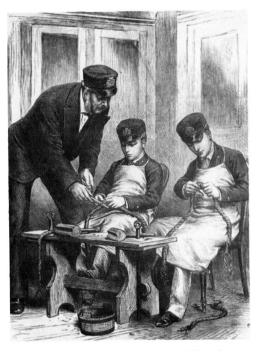

A contemporary postcard of the 'Royal Sailor Boys'. It shows them being taught to splice ropes. (National Maritime Museum)

Prince George also recalled:

> We had a sort of tuck shop on land, up the steep hill; only we weren't allowed to bring any eatables back into the ship, and they used to search you as you came aboard. Well, the big boys used to fag me to bring them back a whole lot of stuff—and I was always found out and got into trouble in addition to having the stuff confiscated. And the worst of it was, it was always my money: they never paid me back—I suppose they thought there was plenty more where that came from, but in point of fact we were only given a shilling a week pocket money, so it meant a lot to me, I can tell you.

But George survived these boyish humiliations and they stood him well in the years to come. The navy's influence upon the young Prince was profound and everlasting. His eldest son later recorded in his *A King's Story* that his father had 'a gruff, bluewater approach to all human problems'.

---

* Recorded by Sir Owen Morshead, January 1932 in *King George V : A Personal Memoir* by John Gore, John Murray, 1941.

George passed out of *Britannia* creditably enough in July 1879 at the age of fourteen, his development as a cadet being described as 'rapid and pronounced'. Prince Eddy, by contrast, was lacking in George's energy and quickness and 'those habits of promptitude and method, of manliness and self-reliance'. His backwardness made him unsuited to a naval career but Mr Dalton believed that the two Princes would benefit by continuing their education together and he persuaded both the Prince of Wales and the Queen to this viewpoint. George and Eddy, it was proposed, should embark on a training cruise around the world with instructors Mr John Lawless and Paymaster G. F. Sceales.

The ship chosen was the 3912-tons screw frigate HMS *Bacchante*, Captain Lord Charles Scott, aboard which the two Princes were quartered in a tiny cabin, communicating with Mr Dalton's, with two swinging cots and their sea chests. Sixteen midshipmen

The screw corvette HMS Bacchante *in which the royal cadets George and Eddy toured the world. (National Maritime Museum)*

were aboard including the captain's own son, all of whom took the icy plunge into the rigours of life at sea in a gunroom.

HMS *Bacchante* sailed from Spithead for the Mediterranean on 17 September 1879. It was the first of three cruises which can be summarized as follows: the first lasted for nearly eight months and took in the Mediterranean and the West Indies; the second was spent with the Channel Fleet and Reserve Squadron, lasted just a few weeks and introduced George and Eddy to Bantry Bay and Vigo; the third—and most important cruise—lasted from 14 September 1880 to 5 August 1882, almost exactly two years and included visits to South America, South Africa, Australia, Japan, China, Singapore, Egypt and the Holy Lands.

The second cruise to the Caribbean was under the command of Uncle Alfred and it was while George was in Bermuda that he officiated at his first ceremonial duty, laying the foundation stone of a Sailor's Home. It was here, too, where a tiny incident occurred which provided an anecdote which has survived a hundred years. The two Princes visited the botanical gardens in Barbados where they sniffed some large lilies so their noses became powdered with yellow pollen. A journalist mistook the pollen and telegraphed the story that they had had their noses tattooed. The report aroused anger at home. The Princess of Wales wrote to George: 'How could you have your impudent snout tattooed? What an *object* you must look, and won't everybody stare at the ridiculous boy with an anchor on his nose!'

It is the third cruise of the *Bacchante* which provides the most interest. We have already read of Prince Louis Battenberg's participation in this cruise aboard the *Inconstant* which together with the *Bacchante* and three other screw corvettes formed the Flying Squadron. The anecdote of the unread telegram which allowed the squadron to reach the Falklands when it was required in South Africa has already been told.

Prince George had by now started on his lifelong habit of keeping a diary: fifty-six years of his life are recorded in twenty-four bound volumes in clear handwriting, assiduously registering the times of rising and going to bed, the state of the barometer, wind direction, the people he met and the engagements he kept. While in South Africa George made a boyish entry regarding one of his shore runs:

'We passed an ostridge farm and saw a good many ostridges.'

On another occasion the Princes, accompanied by the British Governor, visited Cetewayo, King of the Zulus, victor over the British at the battle of Isandhlwano, but loser at Ulundi in 1879. When George met him he was an internee with a small farm to support his family. George wrote:

> He seems a bloodthirsty old chap . . . and said that 'he wanted to wash his spears in the blood of the Boers of the Transvaal' . . . he is 18 stone, heavy in the haunches with enormous thighs and legs . . . and his wives 16 and 17 stone: there are four of them, they are very fine women, all over six feet.

It was an exciting experience for the Princes.

Before the South African problem had been resolved, the Flying Squadron had left Cape Town and set out on its five-week passage to cross the expanse of the Indian Ocean to Australia. Thursday 12 May 1881 is recorded in *The Cruise of HMS* Bacchante*:

> At 5.15 a.m. a sea struck and filled the port cutter in a heavy roll, and she was washed away. Force of the wind 10, and stronger in the squalls; heavy seas running . . . there was nearly a foot or more of water sometimes on the deck. About noon . . . a very heavy roll carried away both davits [of the starboard cutter] which snapped about four feet from the foot and caused her to fall in against the weather mizzen rigging, where she was lashed for the present . . . we were under double-reefed fore and main topsails, foresail and reefed mainsail. This was all the sail we could carry. We split one mainsail and shifted it . . . the sea . . . was literally one mass of white foam boiling and hissing beneath the gale.

The following day it was discovered that the ship's rudder had suffered serious damage; makeshift repairs were made enabling the ship to be handled and when the storm subsided a landfall was made

---

* *The Cruise of HMS* Bacchante *1879-82*, Vols I and II, Ed. by Canon J. N. Dalton, Macmillan & Co., 1886.

in Western Australia and later in the afternoon of 15 May the *Bacchante* was brought to a safe anchorage in St George's Sound, within sight of the township of Albany. There, the Princes transferred to the *Inconstant* while the *Bacchante* underwent permanent repairs, rejoining her later at Sydney and then proceeding on the Far Eastern cruise.

A highlight of this part of the cruise was the visit to Japan and the meeting with the Emperor and Empress of Japan. The thirty-year-old Mikado met the Princes and exchanged pleasantries: Eddy told the Mikado that the Queen had ordered a portrait of herself in oils to be despatched as a token of friendship: and there was much amusement at the spontaneous gift by Eddy of two wallabies from the *Bacchante* to the Empress, which had to be crated and carried ashore by British bluejackets the next day.

The squadron left Japan and began the long haul homewards: Shanghai, Hong Kong, Singapore, then re-crossing the Indian Ocean from Colombo to Suez where the Princes landed on 1 March 1882.

The wonders of the Nile were revealed to the Princes as they steamed up this majestic riverway as far as Luxor: there they toured the ruined temples and sweltered in the heat at the site of ancient Thebes, some of whose important archaelogical discoveries in the Valley of the Kings were still to be unearthed. The Khedive received the Princes and entertained them at Cairo and made sure they wondered at the sight of the Great Pyramids.

The month of April was spent on a tour of the Holy Land and it was near Jerusalem where the Princes camped among the olives that they really were tattooed. George wrote to his mother towards the end of April: 'We have been Tatoed by the same old man that tatoed Papa and the same thing too the 5 crosses. You ask Papa to show his arm.' The Princes also visited Nazareth, Cana of Galilee and the Lake of Gennesaret.

The visit to Greece was a specially happy and affectionate interlude in the world tour; George and Eddy visited their Greek relations: there was Uncle Willy, King George of the Hellenes, the gifted and affectionate Queen Olga of whom George was especially fond, and his cousins.

On leaving the Piraeus the *Bacchante* spent another five weeks in the Mediterranean before heading for home and when the coast of Devon was sighted George wrote with considerable understatement: 'I was glad to see it.' On 5 August 1882 the corvette came to anchor in Cowes Roads. When Queen Victoria saw the two boys a few days later she was delighted at the reunion: 'Georgie', she wrote, 'is much grown. He has still the same bright, merry face as ever.' A few days later George left the *Bacchante* saying farewell to many shipmates of three years, and the ship paid off at the end of August.

The world tour marked an important phase in George's life, for by the time of his return to England in 1882 at the age of eighteen his habits of thought and conduct, his temperament, his affections and prejudices, his whole approach to life, had been shaped in the formative teenage years spent in the Royal Navy.

His next naval appointment came in the summer of 1883 after a brief spell of schooling in Lausanne. His appointment to HMS *Canada* of the North America and West Indies Squadron was a lonely experience for George: there were no tutors, no friends— only Captain Francis Durrant into whose care as governor George had been entrusted by both the Queen and the Prince of Wales. Durrant's instructions were clear; Prince George was to be treated in all respects in the same manner as the other officers: he was to receive no privileges, attend no receptions in his honour; he was to share the harsh life of midshipmen, sleeping in a hammock in a crowded gunroom.

The 2300-ton corvette, built of steel, iron and wood and equipped with both steam and sail, joined the squadron in North America, a squadron commanded by one of the navy's first officers to win the VC—in the Crimea—Vice Admiral Sir John Commerell.

George made time to visit Niagara where he saw the Falls, Ottawa, Montreal, Quebec, Lake Erie where he had some good duck shooting, and Halifax: he danced and made friends, and later played cricket in Bermuda and visited Antigua and Demerara. He returned to England in July 1884 as a newly promoted Sub-Lieutenant.

George was required to attend the Royal Navy College at Greenwich, followed by a gunnery course at HMS *Excellent*, both of which allowed him time to get home to London or to his beloved

Sandringham. While the Prince was at Greenwich Captain B. Currey was appointed his deputy governor. Currey later recalled accompanying George to London and the Prince asking to be allowed to pay the cabman as he had never done so before: Currey gave George the fare and a shilling tip.

The gunnery and pilotage course at HMS *Excellent* where the redoubtable Captain J. A. (Jacky) Fisher was in command, and Lieutenant Percy Scott, the famous gunnery expert, was an instructor, lasted till October 1885 and George gained first-class passes in seamanship, gunnery and torpedo work. Captain Fisher wrote: 'Prince George only lost his first class at Pilotage by 20 marks. The reason is that one of his examiners, an old salt-horse sailor, didn't think it would do to let him fancy he knew all about it.'

No time was lost in securing George's next appointment. Captain Harry Neale Stephenson, captain of the *Carysfort* during the *Bacchante* cruise, equerry to the Prince of Wales and long-time friend of the royal family, had exchanged the confines of court ritual for the rigours of command at sea.

The *Thunderer*, in fact, was a poor choice of ship. She was old, having been launched at Pembroke in 1872, mounted four massive 38-ton muzzle-loading turret guns, one of which misfired and burst during gunnery exercises in the Sea of Marmara, killing eight of the crew. The ship had deteriorated with age, to such an extent that— at best—a major refit was due and at worst the ship needed scrapping. The overdue refit was carried out in Malta where George's uncle, Prince Alfred was C-in-C, and there Captain Stephenson together with George was temporarily transferred to the *Dreadnought* whose commander was Prince Louis of Battenberg, thus completing a royal triumvirate of sailor princes serving at Malta at the same time.

For relaxation in Malta, George's interests were much like any other young naval officer's with private means. He played polo on the Marsa, a sport much enjoyed later by Prince Philip, Earl Mountbatten and Prince Charles; he rode and picnicked ashore, spent much time at San Antonio Palace with his aunt and girl cousins; he played billiards in the evening at the Union Club in the Strada Reale and it is possible that it was here that he was influenced by his uncle's hobby of stamp collecting, which he took up most

Since earliest childhood Prince George had been especially close to his mother, Princess Alexandra, Princess of Wales. (Her Majesty the Queen)

enthusiastically and which became a fascinating pastime for him—and his son, King George VI—in later life.

He accompanied his uncle on a visit to the Sultan of Turkey in October 1886, an occasion marked by the bestowal of magnificent gifts: George received a white Arab horse and a jewelled cigarette case. Other visits were made to Beyrouth and to Alexandria where the Khedive visited the *Dreadnought* as she was coaling and was astonished when he had presented to him a coal-grimed youngster, grandson of the great Queen and Empress.

It was at about this time that George first grew a full set. He sent a photograph of himself to Queen Victoria. 'I daresay' he wrote to her, 'that you will think that my beard has altered me rather.' Mother did not entirely approve and brother Eddy thought it made George look so much older. 'Old Curzon', he added encouragingly, 'has taken off his and looks much better.'

George was always anxious to please the family. He longed for and always expressed affection, especially to his mother who was forever Mother-dear in his correspondence and with whom he retained an intimate, almost child-like relationship. He found in his mother the confidante for his thoughts: to her he threw discretion to the winds and opened his heart.

George also expressed a love for England. 'How delightful', he noted in his diary for 16 June 1887, 'to be in dear old England again . . . Dearest Papa, darling Mother-dear, Eddy and sisters and George of Greece came to meet me . . .' His return to England was to celebrate Queen Victoria's Golden Jubilee and the reunion in London reads like a geneaology table of Europe's royal families: it included the Kings of Greece, Denmark and Saxony; the Prince and Princess William of Prussia; Prince Henry of Prussia; Don Carlos of Portugal; the Grand Duke of Weimar; Prince Louis of Baden; the Crown Prince Rudolph of Austria; Prince Antoine d'Orleans and the Infanta Eulalie; princes and dukes and relations of Coburg, of Battenberg, of Hohenlohe; Prince Louis of Bavaria. The celebrations in the summer both at court and in the streets of villages and towns throughout the country were manifestations of the affection of everyone for the ageing Queen Victoria, especially in London where George among all the other grandsons and sons rode before the Queen to the Abbey amid 'deafening applause'.

George returned to Malta in August and rejoined the *Dreadnought* soon to be commanded by Captain Noel Digby. George described the ship without Captain Stephenson as 'like Hamlet without Hamlet'. Christmas of this jubilee year was spent happily enough with the Duke and Duchess of Edinburgh and his cousins at San Antonio and soon after the festivities the *Dreadnought* sailed to Salamis Bay for torpedo exercises and this enabled George to spend ten splendid days' leave at Athens. His letters home and his diary faithfully record his affection for Uncle Willy (born Prince William of Denmark), Aunt Olga (Grand Duchess Olga Constantinovna, niece of the Tsar Alexander II) and his cousins.

Later in the year George was aboard the Duke's flagship when she made ceremonial visits to some Greek islands and to Spain. Some of his experiences are recorded in a letter to Captain Stephenson with whom he maintained a regular correspondence:

> Everything went off very well at Barcelona . . . but the only thing was we were by far the weakest squadron, which I think is simply disgraceful . . . I saw a 'bull fight' one day at Algeciras. I must say I never saw a more disgusting sight and I never wish to see another one. We went from there to Malaga and remained there four days, I stopped aboard to keep watch while the others went off to Grenada. Then we went to Valencia, touching at Alicante . . .

Prince George then accompanied the Duke and Duchess of Edinburgh to Madrid where they saw all the famous sights. Before the year end George was on his way home overland across Europe to Sandringham where he enjoyed excellent shooting, making up for the two previous Christmasses spent abroad.

But in a few weeks he was back at sea aboard the *Orantes* on passage to Gibraltar: 'I feel horribly homesick and miss darling Mother-dear and sisters too dreadfully,' he wrote, but he was also horribly seasick, an affliction he never overcame in all the years he spent at sea.

At Gibraltar he joined the *Northumberland* (Captain Darwin) which was attached to the Channel Squadron, operating between Gibraltar, Tangier, Vigo and Corunna.

In July, George was appointed to Torpedo Boat No 79—in command. He later described it as the happiest day of his life, albeit he was commissioning a vessel of only 75 tons. 'A Yarrow boat,' he recorded, '128 feet long and goes 19 knots. Thorp is my Sub . . . Mr Elliott is my gunner . . . and a very good man.' It was a proud

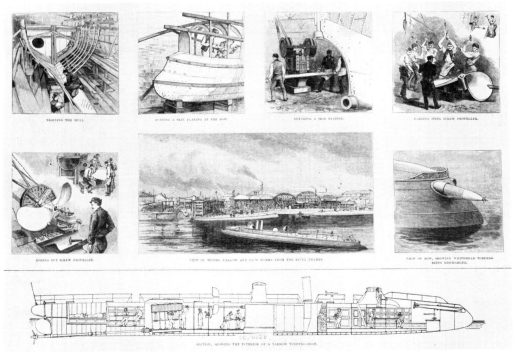

Prince George's first command Torpedo Boat No 79, had been built by Yarrow & Co at their Poplar works on the River Thames. (National Maritime Museum)

time for Prince George. Very soon Torpedo Boat No 79 attended naval exercises at Spithead in honour of Kaiser Wilhelm II who had succeeded to the German throne only a year earlier at the age of twenty-nine on the death of his father the Emperor Frederick. It was an impressive display of naval might by more than one hundred men-of-war.

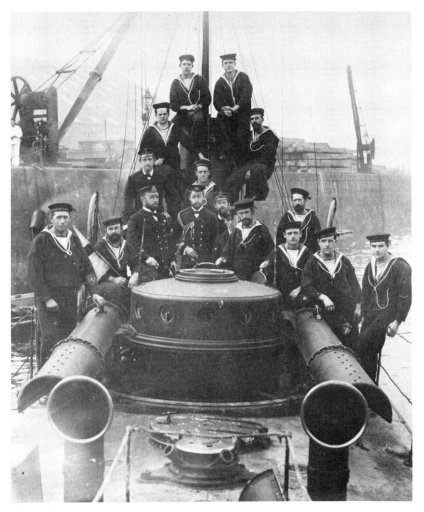

Prince George with most of his crew aboard Torpedo Boat No 79. (Her Majesty the Queen)

Almost immediately afterwards Prince George was despatched with other units of the fleet to Western Ireland for further exercises. The weather was stormy with a head wind and nasty sea which shook up the torpedo boats and George suffered terribly again from sickness. In the course of the exercises he succeeded in passing a tow across to TB No *41* and towing her off to safety after she had broken down in Lough Swilly and was in a perilous position on a lee shore. It was a piece of seamanship which 'would have reflected credit on an officer of far wider experience than His Royal Highness'. On de-commissioning the ship at Portsmouth George thanked all members of the crew and presented everyone of them with a photograph of himself and a golden sovereign.

Prince George renewed his acquaintanceship with his cousin Kaiser Wilhelm in 1890 after completing a gunnery course at HMS *Excellent*. He and Eddy made an official state visit to Berlin then went on to Coburg and Stuttgart before returning home to take command of the first-class gunboat HMS *Thrush*, lying at Chatham and destined for the North America Station. She was a modern screw gunboat of 805 tons with a top speed of about 13 knots. Her crew numbered seven officers and fifty-seven men and her main armament comprised four 4-inch guns.

George took the *Thrush* to Devonport where she was ordered to tow TB No *70* to Gibraltar. It was a hazardous operation as George described it to Captain Stephenson:

We were in the middle of the Bay [of Biscay] when suddenly without warning our engines brought up all standing. We then discovered that the slide and eccentric rods were both bent nearly double; lucky to say it was a dead calm at the time, and I made the TB get up steam and remain by us all night. We were quite helpless. We proceeded at once to put the spare rods in and with the whole engine room staff working all night we were ready in exactly 12 hours . . . It then came on to blow hard from the southwest with a heavy sea and the poor boat was having a very bad time of it . . . we knocked about a good deal all night and needless to say I was seasick but the ship is an excellent sea boat and we took very little water in. We stopped at Ferrol for two days

Opposite *Captain Horatio Nelson painted by John Francis Rigaud in 1781. Prince William thought him the 'youngest-looking captain' he had ever seen. (National Maritime Museum)*

CAPT. HORATIO NELSON
1781.

HMS Thrush *appears in the column on the right in this painting by Edward de Martino of the Channel Squadron. (National Maritime Museum)*

... then arrived safely at Gibraltar where more permanent repairs were effected.

The *Thrush* called at Las Palmas for coal then completed the 2750-mile voyage to Bermuda in seventeen days after suffering the ordeal of rolling interminably and experiencing high engine room temperatures up to 140° F. Prince George took the *Thrush* to Halifax to join the flag of Vice Admiral George Watson who noted that the new arrival was 'a happy ship, efficiently manned and commanded'.

Prince George remained on the station for nearly a year and engrossed himself in sporting activities ashore, shooting woodcock, fishing for salmon, playing polo and sometimes golf, improving his tennis, dancing and interspersing these activities with the occasional ceremonial duty, including the opening of the Industrial Exhibition in Jamaica in January 1891. His letters and diary entries during this period became more forceful, his conclusions more resolute; he seemed to be growing in stature, gaining in confidence, the discipline, training and hard work of the navy seeming to help mould his character, and the responsibility and ordeals of command having helped make the man. At the end of July 1891, on his return to Plymouth, he recorded with methodical precision that the *Thrush* had steamed 2479.3 miles from Halifax to Plymouth in a time of 309 hours 47 minutes with a mean daily distance run of 192

Opposite Top *Sailors carousing in the Long Assembly Room at Portsmouth. They are celebrating receipt of prize money from the capture of Spanish gold. (National Maritime Museum).* Bottom *Thomas Rowlandson's aquatint shows a midshipman of 1799, dressed as Prince William required. (National Maritime Museum)* knots and a total coal usage of 85 tons 19 cwt. On return to England he was promoted Commander and the *Thrush* was paid off.

While George was on the North America Station his brother Eddy reached the age of twenty-six and was created Duke of Clarence and Avondale, a title which George thought 'an awful mouthful'. Talk of marriage for both Princes was now being bandied about and the names of prospective brides, daughters of Europe's royal families, were considered for the eligible bachelors. It was Eddy who first took the steps to matrimony. On 3 December 1891 his proposal of marriage was accepted by the twenty-four-year-old Princess Mary of Teck, but by a cruel stroke of fate he fell ill with influenza, pneumonia set in and on 14 January 1892 he died.

Prince George was stunned by the bereavement and desolate at his own personal loss of the person who had been closest to him throughout his life. But, more importantly, Eddy's death now made George the heir presumptive and the whole of his present life-style became threatened. Five months later he was created Duke of York, Earl of Inverness and Baron Killarney and after taking his seat in the House of Lords he resumed his naval duties.

At the end of June he took command of the 3400-tons armoured cruiser HMS *Melampus* for the summer manœuvres. On 2 July, with his old friend Canon Dalton as guest, he took the cruiser to Lough Swilly in heavy weather for torpedo firing and other exercises. Later, as a unit of the Red Squadron, the *Melampus* took part in more exercises in Tor Bay and later still the manœuvres continued in Mounts Bay and then in the Irish Sea, all in unseasonable weather; days of a heaving ship and violent seasickness induced George to write: 'Hate the whole thing . . . feel quite done up.' From George's own accounts the exercises seem to have been tiresome in the extreme with endless mistakes, not least by the flagship. It had been an unhappy episode in his naval career which now appeared to be in jeopardy.

For two months that autumn George was sent to Germany to the Black Forest university town of Heidelberg, to improve his German under the rather eccentric Professor Ilne. The setting was idyllic: a charming villa set among vineyards and terraced gardens with a view over the River Neckar and the beautiful town. But all this seems to have been lost on George. He found it 'beastly dull' there and made no bones about describing German as 'this rotten language which I find very difficult'.

While in Germany George attended army manœuvres and later paid a visit to the Grand Duke and Duchess of Baden at Karlsruhe before returning home. What this visit exposed, he realized, was his ignorance of politics and matters of state. With the Queen's approval and with the help of his father the Prince of Wales, George began to occupy himself with such matters and very soon he had met and dined with the great Liberal statesmen, Mr Gladstone and Mr Asquith. He began to attend debates in the House of Commons and even recorded that Gladstone's two and a quarter hour speech before a crammed House introducing the Home Rule Bill was 'beautiful' and a wonderful achievement for a man of eighty-three.

The newly promoted captain had things other than politics on his mind that spring. On 3 May 1893 he proposed marriage to his late brother's fiancée, Princess Mary of Teck and they were married two months later in the Chapel Royal at St James' Palace, he wearing the uniform of a naval captain.

The Duke and new Duchess of York spent their honeymoon at York Cottage on the Sandringham estate which he loved so dearly.

George had only one more brief spell of active service in the Royal Navy and this was to occur after nearly six years ashore, living the life of a private almost obscure country gentleman. He assumed command of the cruiser *Crescent* for some weeks exercising around Ireland and Scotland before joining the Channel Squadron at Kirkwall. George's old tutor and shipmate, Canon Dalton was again happy to be invited to accompany his old pupil. The exercises were, in fact, the end of George's naval career and when he was piped ashore, it was to be for the last time as a serving officer.

His naval service had spanned an amazing period of naval development from the 1880s, when the Royal Navy was by far the largest in the world, adopting as policy the Two-Power Standard whereby the Royal Navy maintained a fleet double the size of any two European navies. By 1897 the Royal Navy comprised 332 vessels manned by 90,000 volunteers: France had 95 vessels, Russia 86, Germany 68, the USA 56 and Italy 53. But quantity failed to compensate for quality. Perhaps half of the RN ships were obsolete,

Prince George (later George V) is seen here as a Vice Admiral with his two eldest sons—Edward (later Edward VIII) and Albert (later George VI). His father, Edward VII, is shown as an Admiral of the Fleet although, unlike his son, he was never an active sailor. (Her Majesty the Queen)

adequate to perform the world's policing with ceremony and pageantry but lacking in the necessary *matériel* and skills which characterized Nelson's band of brothers; gunnery was rarely exercised, firing guns blistered gleaming paintwork and smartness was crucial to a ship's appearance. It needed the Fishers and Percy Scotts and Battenbergs to bring about a significant change and it was they who emerged, took charge, and heralded the new navy of the twentieth century.

George retired from this service to York Cottage and raised a fine family of six children. He duly received promotion to flag rank in 1901, to full Admiral four years later and to Admiral of the Fleet on 7 May 1910, the day after his accession to the throne.

Throughout the twenty-six years of his eventful reign, scarred deeply by the First World War, the industrial unrest of the twenties and the tragic unemployment of the thirties, the steadfast British monarchy, as Nicholson reminds us, witnessed the disappearance of five emperors, eight kings and eighteen minor dynasties. King George, dubbed 'George the Good' by some, brought to his kingship many of the qualities imbued in him during his long years of naval service—a simple, devout, disciplined, even selfless service to the people of the nation and of the Empire over which he reigned.

8

The Windsor Princes

THE PRINCE who inherited the throne yet never wore the crown was born in the late evening of 23 June 1894 in the splendid Georgian house called White Lodge which graced Richmond Park. Prince Edward Albert Christian George Andrew Patrick David—but always known in the family as David—was the first born son of Princess May and the twenty-nine-year-old Captain Prince George, the great-grandson of the ageing Queen Victoria.

Prince Edward's birth was acclaimed throughout the vast British Empire, the most powerful empire that the world had known, embracing a quarter of the earth's surface, for the infant prince became the third in direct line of succession to the throne which for nearly fifty-seven years had belonged to Queen Victoria. And when, in due passage of time, Edward ascended this same throne forty-two years later, most of the stable, glittering monarchies of Victoria's day had gone for ever, and boisterous dictators strutted across the fragile European stage.

Edward was born into the finely regulated life of the English Court and into the isolation of York Cottage at Sandringham and it was here that the Duke and Duchess of York—as his father and mother were properly called—bore the rest of their children: Bertie in 1895, Mary in 1897, Henry in 1900, George in 1902 and John in 1905. Bertie was to become King George VI; Mary the Princess Royal; Henry the Duke of Gloucester; George the Duke of Kent; John was to die as a youngster of fourteen.

Bertie's life was to be marked by a number of handicaps, not least the inheritance of an unwanted crown from his older brother, and it seems as if providence had marked him with a stigma for he chose to be born on the very anniversary of the Prince Consort's

This 1900 photograph of the young Princes—Edward standing, Albert on the cushion and Henry on his great-grandmother's lap—became a popular postcard. Seated on the wicker chair is Princess Mary and a nanny crouches out of sight to give support to Queen Victoria's arm as she cradles the baby. (Her Majesty the Queen)

death, and, incidentally, of the death of Princess Alice, a day of sorrow for Queen Victoria and therefore the royal family. Bertie was to suffer shyness, a sad affliction for a Prince in the public eye, but worse still he had always to strive to overcome a slight stammer that stayed with him all his life.

The new century brought dramatic change: the unhappy years of the Boer War had finally been brought to an end; Victoria's glorious years gave way to the new Edwardian era and the country had a new Prince of Wales. Change came about, too, for the two Princes Edward and Bertie. The Prince of Wales, set in his ideas, had decided upon an education for the Princes precisely along the lines of his own upbringing; home tutors would be employed until the boys were old enough to join the navy as cadets.

The tutor who came to York Cottage in the spring of 1902 was the thirty-nine-year-old Henry Peter Hansell, a bachelor schoolmaster of modest scholastic attainment at Oxford, a keen golfer, footballer and crack rifle shot. Mr Hansell wished the boys should go to a preparatory school but the Prince of Wales dismissed the idea peremptorily: 'My brother [Eddy] and I never went to a prep school: the navy will teach David all he needs to know.'

Mr Hansell strived resourcefully to create a boarding school atmosphere at York Cottage for the two youngsters by organizing a schoolroom with standard pattern school desks and seats, blackboard and wall maps. The morning routine was devoted to scholastic pursuits, the afternoon to walking, sporting activities and military-style drilling. The Princes experienced an isolated upbringing, rarely mixed with youngsters of their own age and were subjected to the strict disciplines imposed by a Victorian father who believed implicitly in high standards of endeavour, of self-discipline and of moral responsibility. The Duke of Windsor, recalling these early days, described his father with the telling phrase 'He believed in God, in the invincibility of the Royal Navy and the essential rightness of whatever was British.' It is inevitable that he tried to instill into his sons these very beliefs and faiths; inevitable, too, that he should wish his sons to do well in preparation for their entry into the navy.

Edward, the elder brother, became due to sit his competitive examination for a cadetship in 1907 at the age of twelve and a half. The oral interview was conducted by a panel of admirals and schoolmasters. Edward recalled two of the questions asked—

whether he was afraid of the dark and the name of his favourite author. He impressed the panel sufficiently to earn selection for the written examinations, a three-day ordeal in a public hall in London where one hundred candidates competed for the sixty-seven places available in the new term at the Royal Naval College at Osborne.

Edward passed creditably which pleased both himself and his father who personally supervised his son's fitting out for a uniform by a man from Gieves. Two years later, in 1909, Bertie followed suit and passed both the oral and written examinations for entry into the navy despite Mr Hansell's report to the Prince of Wales: 'He has reached a good standard all round, but one must remember that he is at present a scatterbrain and it is perfectly impossible to say how he will fare at Osborne.'

Osborne House, on the Isle of Wight, had been a favourite home of Queen Victoria but few of her family shared her affection for the place, and on her death King Edward promptly disposed of it by giving the Osborne Estate of over 2000 acres to the nation as a con-valescent home for officers. Admiral Sir John Fisher suggested using the building and the site as a naval college where cadets would undergo the first two years of their training, finishing off with another two at the newly designed college at Dartmouth whose foundation stone King Edward had laid in March 1902. The King approved Fisher's proposals and within weeks a collection of single-storey buildings had been constructed in the spacious grounds of Osborne House to provide dormitories, gunrooms, class rooms and officers' quarters together with a central great barn-like hall called Nelson which served as a quarterdeck and place of general assembly. On the huge oak cross beam supporting the organ gallery were large brass letters spelling out Nelson's famous motto: THERE IS NOTHING THE NAVY CANNOT DO. The new college was formally opened by the King and the Prince of Wales on 4 August 1903.

Cadet HRH Prince Edward of Wales was the first royal sailor to attend Osborne and he was to find his royal family background a handicap in the boisterous company of hundreds of cadets, where senior boys persecuted the new entrants. Royal rank was no safe-guard and Prince Edward came in for his fair share of chastisement at the hands of the sixth termers at the college. The first indignity accorded him was just before quarters one evening when he was cornered and made to stand to attention while a bottle of red ink was poured over his head which ran down his neck and ruined a shirt. Mr Hansell's years of teaching failed to provide a solution to the dilemma of missing quarters or reporting his assailants. Prince Edward missed quarters, was rebuked and earned three days 1A punishment—alternately spending leisure hours doubling round the stableblock with a heavy rod across his shoulders and staring vacantly at the wall in the seamanship room. On another occasion a sash window was forced down on his neck—as a reminder of the fate of Charles I and the method of dealing with recalcitrant royals.

In command of the college was Captain Edwin Alexander-Sinclair, responsible for administration, discipline and the teaching of naval history. He had a staff of twenty-seven term officers, mostly lieutenants in their mid-twenties. A headmaster with a teaching staff of thirty-two conducted normal tutorials. The new entry was allocated to two of the twelve dormitories, each pair taking the name of a famous admiral; Prince Edward's was Exmouth, and this was the name given to the term. Each term was divided into port and starboard watches—starboard for the brightest boys. Prince Edward was in the port watch.

He found the transition from royal residence to the stark realities of an iron bed and a sea chest and looking out for himself without a man Friday to fetch and carry for him especially hard. But with the resilience of youth Edward quickly adapted to the harsh routines and soon learned the basic rule that there was only one way to do anything—the navy way.

But the end-of-term report to his father showed it to have been an undistinguished term: the second term showed no improvement so a maths teacher was engaged to cram Edward, a tactic which earned a better report at the end of the third term but so fearful was Edward when summoned to his father's library to learn of his term's results that he burst into tears before hearing the verdict. 'Come David,' the Prince of Wales admonished mildly, 'this is no way for a naval cadet to act. Besides, you have quite a good report this time, and I am pleased with the progress you have made.'

Edward's reward for his endeavours at Osborne was the cadets' weekly pocket money of one shilling paid out to the queuing cadets at noon on Saturdays. No sooner had the money been paid than a rush was made to the canteen where threepence would buy a bagful of sweets, stuffed dates, fruit and ice cream from the old naval pensioner who ran the canteen. But by mid-week the money had run out and so hungry did Edward feel one day that he feigned illness with the hope of securing a meal from the matron. She saw through his malingering. He burst into tears and confessed his deception and hunger. He recalled with pleasure that the matron admonished him fiercely—then fed him with buttered eggs, bread and jam.

The two years at Osborne ended and in May 1909 Prince Edward moved to the RN College at Dartmouth. This splendid new building displayed a permanency that Osborne always seemed to lack and its commanding position on a steep hill overlooking the tranquil and deep-wooded reaches of the sparkling River Dart, in one of the most beautiful spots of England, made it a memorable experience for every cadet who attended there.

Prince Edward's first impressions of the new college were not favourable. From being a senior sixth-termer at Osborne, he now reverted to being a new entrant and was subjected to renewed indignities and persecutions, but he soon grew to appreciate the manliness of Dartmouth. The young Prince was growing up, the cadets were treated less like children, firm friendships were being formed, he attended some of the Saturday night dances, proved himself a useful oarsman in the college regattas and—like his great-nephew Prince Charles—enjoyed amateur dramatics, appearing in a college production of *HMS Pinafore*.

Edward left Dartmouth, denied the final training cruise and therefore his midshipman's coveted tabs, in order to assist in the 1911 coronation ceremonies in his new role of Prince of Wales. After his investiture the King arranged for Edward to go to sea in the coal-burning battleship *Hindustan*, commanded by Captain Henry H. Campbell, an old friend of the family. Edward was to discover, however, that the genial guest at Sandringham was not the same man as the captain with a deck under his feet. 'I was under the instruction of the officers, warrant officers and chief petty officers responsible for every part of ship,' Edward recorded. 'I kept watch

Although he had to retire from the navy while still a midshipman Prince Edward continued to rise in rank and is seen here in a slightly dishevelled uniform bidding goodbye to his brothers Albert and Henry before setting off, with his cousin, Dickie Mountbatten, on a tour of the Empire (March 1920). (Broadlands Archives)

at sea and in harbour. I learned how to run a picket boat; I served in a turret during battle practice, and was taught to read flag signals by the Chief Yeoman . . . I enjoyed the experience immensely. Though I was the junior midshipman in the gunroom . . . all the others . . . treated me with more compassion than I had received when I joined Osborne . . . I . . . looked forward to the dirty, back-breaking job of coaling ship for the cigarettes I was allowed to smoke on these occasions . . .'

King George sent for Edward after three months of sea service and announced that his naval career, barely started, must end.

* * *

Meanwhile Bertie's scholastic attainments at Osborne were even less impressive than Edward's; he was consistently bottom of his class or near bottom, despite the efforts of the new commanding officer, Captain Arthur Christian, of Grenville's term officer, Lieutenant William Phipps and of tutor Mr James Watt. Bertie's father rebuked him sternly: '. . . you don't seem to take your work at all seriously, nor do you appear to be very keen about it. My dear boy, this will not do . . . unless you now put your shoulder to the wheel and really try to do your best to work hard you will have no chance of passing your examinations.'

However, Bertie did achieve entry into Dartmouth where he soon began a lifetime's friendship with Surgeon Lieutenant Greig, later Group Captain Sir Louis Greig, Comptroller of Bertie's household when he became Duke of York.

Bertie's two years at Dartmouth were marked by a deplorable scholastic record to the despair of his tutors. Mr Watt was at his wit's end when he wrote to Mr Hansell on the occasion of Bertie's being placed sixty-eighth out of sixty-eight: 'I am afraid there is no disguising to you the fact that Prince Albert has gone a mucker . . . I am afraid that their Majesties will be very disappointed.'

Bertie was fortunate in having as term officer Lieutenant Henry Spencer-Cooper (Scoops to the cadets) who encouraged him among other things to ride, to beagle and specially to play tennis—left-handedly—a natural trait which tutors had despised for years, probably contributing to his stammer and backwardness. His two years were also marked by a number of royal occasions, notably the coronation of his father in June 1911, the investiture of his brother as Prince of Wales and the Coronation Naval Review at Spithead.

In May 1912 the King held another naval review—off Weymouth—and Cadet Prince Albert found himself with intense delight aboard the Royal Yacht in the company of the First Lord of the Admiralty, Winston Churchill, the First Sea Lord, Prince Louis of Battenberg and the Prime Minister, Mr Asquith. A fleet of 28 battleships, 3 battle-cruisers, 11 heavy cruisers, many flotillas of destroyers and 50 submarines were drawn up in six precise lines, in impressive, solemn array, ready for inspection by King George V.

Bertie was specially excited by two incidents at the Review. He accompanied his father and the First Lord into the confines of the submarine *D 4* which was commanded by Lieutenant Dunbar-Nasmith, later Admiral Sir Martin Dunbar-Nasmith VC, KCB, who distinguished himself in the submarine *E 11* in an exploit in the Sea of Marmara. Bertie wrote an account of his trip in the *D 4*: 'We steamed out past the breakwater. There we dived and went about three miles under water which took about 20 minutes. When we came up again there was a thick fog, but it cleared off very quickly and we returned to the Yacht.' It was a revolutionary experience both for the King and his son.

That evening the dinner was a glittering affair: in addition to the young Winston Churchill and the elegant Battenburg, there dined four admirals all to gain renown in the rapidly advancing war: Jellicoe, Beatty, Sturdee of Coronel and Cradock of the Falkland Islands. It was Bertie's first meeting with Churchill, the man with whom he was to work so closely throughout World War II. Bertie's return to Dartmouth must have seemed a bit humdrum by comparison.

Back at college his scholastic abilities displayed a consistent mediocrity enlivened now and then by pranks such as the incident when, with sixteen other cadets, he fired off illicit fireworks on Guy Fawkes Night for which he earned 'six of the best'. Bertie always harboured a sense of injustice over this punishment because the cane broke on the fourth stroke and he considered he should not have received the remaining two. At another time he helped his friends to drive a flock of sheep into a Saturday night dance after the lights had been doused.

In his last months at Dartmouth Bertie grew noticeably in stature and many of the later qualities he was to display in kingship were becoming evident: he was generous and loyal, unfailingly considerate to others; he never shirked a job nor gave up easily; he always retained a sense of fun and, perhaps most importantly, the navy engendered in him as in Lord Louis Mountbatten, Philip, the Duke of Edinburgh and Charles, the Prince of Wales, that common touch so valuable to members of the royal family. The final judgement on Bertie by his captain at Dartmouth summed it up in one brief, devastating sentence: 'I think he will do.'

The coveted white collar patches and dirk denoting the rank of midshipman only came to Bertie on completion of a training cruise in foreign waters. He joined the 9800-ton cruiser HMS *Cumberland* at Devonport in January 1913 for the purpose of translating the four years of theory and college classroom learning into the practicalities of seamanship and ship-handling and navigation, of obedience and responsibility. The broadening experience of the cruise was marred by Bertie's seasickness, for, like his father, this handicap was to remain with him throughout his sea-time.

The cruise lasted nearly six months and included visits to Tenerife, St Lucia, Trinidad, Barbados, Martinique, San Domingo, Puerto Rico, Jamaica, Havana, Bermuda, Halifax, Quebec, St John's in Newfoundland and Plymouth.

At many of the ports of call he was expected to undertake public duties. At Tenerife he drove through the brightly decorated town as a symbol of monarchy accompanied by his commanding officer, Captain Aubrey Smith, and the British Consul. In the West Indies the clamour of the people and their acclamation was more intense. In Jamaica he opened a new wing of the Kingston Yacht Club, the main building of which had been opened by his father twelve years earlier. It was a stammering ordeal but a dogged performance. Bertie resorted to the ploy of asking a colleague of similar build to stand-in for him to acknowledge the cheers and waving on engagements when no speaking was involved.

From the Caribbean, the *Cumberland* took the Prince to Canada. He brought home stories of the enormous energy manifested by the Canadians, and the rugged and virile scenery of the landscape; he steamed up the wide St Lawrence estuary, beyond Quebec to Montreal, he wondered at the enormity of the Great Lakes, sailed through the beauty of the Thousand Isles and shot the rapids at Long Sault. From Goat Island he saw the thundering magnificence of the Niagara Falls. 'Some of us', he recorded in his diary for 6 June 1913, 'went under the falls which was a curious experience. We took off all our clothes and put on flannels and oilskins . . . The spray is tremendous and soaks you absolutely. When we were actually under the falls we could neither see nor breathe, because the water and spray hits you full in the face and you can only gasp for breath . . . Afterwards I went with a few cadets under the Horseshoe Falls on the Canadian side . . . We struck a rock while shooting the Long Sault Rapids but no harm was done.'

Cumberland returned to her home port early in July and the King was delighted to see the change in Albert when the youngster arrived home on leave. He appeared much improved in self-

Midshipman Prince Albert aboard the Collingwood. *(Imperial War Museum)*

confidence, less tongue-tied than before: in short, he had grown up quite noticeably. When next the King saw Albert's term officer he greeted him: 'Thank you,' he said simply. 'I am pleased with the boy.'

On 15 September 1913 Prince Albert was promoted to midshipman and formally embarked on what he expected to be a lifetime's career but, like his father's, it was to be cut short.

His first sea-going appointment was to HMS *Collingwood*, Captain James Ley. She was a 19,800-ton battleship, the flagship of Vice Admiral Sir Stanley Colville, commanding the First Battle Squadron of the Home Fleet. Colville was an old shipmate of King George's having served with him aboard both the *Canada* and the *Alexandra* in 1888. Aboard the battleship Bertie soon learnt that a 'snotty' was regarded as the lowest form of life, with few privileges, a multitude of duties, many in the form of 'fagging' and much responsibility. For these duties, the midshipman was awarded a sea chest and hammock space in the flat outside the gunroom.

The First Battle Squadron sailed from Devonport to join in manoeuvres in the Mediterranean and then to cruise in Aegean waters. During the cruise the squadron visited Gibraltar, Majorca, Malta, Alexandria, Salamis Bay, Athens, Naples, Toulon and Barcelona before returning to Devonport.

In Alexandria the C-in-C, Admiral Sir Berkeley Milne and Sir Stanley Colville were invited to stay with Lord Kitchener in Cairo, taking with them Prince Albert and another midshipman. Kitchener sought every political advantage in the intrigue of Middle East diplomacy and ensured that Abbas II, the Khedive of Egypt, visited the British Agency to be presented to the son of King George V. The two mids were given a conducted tour of the sights and at the top of the Great Pyramid Bertie saw the scratched initials AE made by his grandfather fifty years earlier.

The visit to Salamis Bay to meet the Greek royal family was marred somewhat for Bertie by a severe cold but he recovered sufficiently to go ashore. He wrote home: 'I saw Uncle Tino and Aunt Sophie and the cousins and I went with George and Alexander to see the Acropolis and museums . . . After tea I motored down to the Piraeus with Aunt Sophie and returned to the ship in the barge.'

Christmas Day was spent aboard *Collingwood* in fine warm

weather, riding at anchor in Gibraltar harbour and a few days later Bertie was reunited with his family at Sandringham. The new year of 1914 found Bertie back in the battleship's gunroom and on 28 June when news of the assassination of the Archduke Franz Ferdinand was received, it caused little stir aboard *Collingwood* as she lay off Brighton in warm sunshine. The dreadful repercussions of the Sarajevo incident took simmering weeks to cast their sombre shadow over Britain. The Archduke, incidentally, had been a guest of King George at Windsor only a few months earlier.

A Test Mobilization of the navy had been called for in July 1914 and on the 17th and 18th of that month the King reviewed the fleet at Spithead, Prince Albert joined his father aboard the royal yacht, *Victoria and Albert*, and dined with no less than sixteen admirals. The next day—Sunday 18th—Bertie was back aboard the *Collingwood* and the mighty fleet took six hours to steam past the royal yacht. Some days later as Austria declared war on Serbia the battle squadrons of the Royal Navy under the command of the First Sea Lord, Prince Louis of Battenberg, were ordered to their war stations at Scapa Flow. A few days later Germany declared war on Russia and then war engulfed Britain: an era had come to an end.

Prince Albert was soon to realize that war at sea entailed endless hours of boredom in a turret, his duty station. It was here, in this turret, that two years later he was to experience one of the highlights of his formative years, his participation in the clash of two giant fleets in a battle which the British called Jutland and the Germans Skagerak.

During those two years Bertie suffered recurrent and persistent bouts of stomach and intestinal ailments including an operation for appendicitis. Recuperation on sick leave kept the young officer ashore for months and for a time he was engaged on temporary appointment to the Operations Division of the Admiralty. He rejoined the *Collingwood* after passing his examination for sub-lieutenant and was a patient aboard his ship in the sick bay yet again when the battleship sailed from the Firth of Forth. The prospect of action brought a miraculous cure in Bertie: he left his sickbed, hurriedly dressed and reported for duty in his turret.

By the spring of 1916 there was unrest within the German navy. Admiral Reinhold von Scheer took command of the High Seas

Fleet and roused it from its apathy. The years of peacetime tax burdens to equip the nation with a fleet called for a return—other than just the success of the unrestricted U-boat warfare. Justification for the fleet, retaliation for the increasing severity of the British blockade and a need to revitalize flagging German spirits resulted in more aggressive naval activity. Von Scheer himself developed an audacious plan for Hipper's battle-cruisers to lure the Grand Fleet, in particular Sir David Beatty's battle-cruisers from Rosyth, to steam to intercept Hipper's force, only to run into a concentration of U-boats. But Hipper's battle-cruisers were not to be alone; he was to form the spearhead, sailing towards the Skagerak, with the main fleet giving distant cover off the Jutland coast.

The British Admiralty were well aware of the large-scale enemy movements and planned to encourage a meeting of Beatty's and Hipper's battle-cruisers and Beatty in his flagship the *Lion* led his battle-cruisers—including the *Collingwood*—from Rosyth on the evening of 30 May. Jellicoe's battleships left Scapa in support. But neither High Command realized the full extent of the other's commitment with the result that by noon on the 31st immense forces were converging on each other for a clash of fleets the like of which had never been seen before.

Beatty had six battle-cruisers supported by four new battleships under Rear Admiral Evan Thomas, some light cruisers and destroyers. As Beatty ran south in search of Hipper's five battle-cruisers and accompanying light cruisers and destroyers now in contact with the scouting HMS *Galatea*, he left Evan Thomas far behind. Battle was joined between the two opposing fleets and fearful duels erupted with extremely accurate fire from Hipper's ships. The inadequacy of the British ships' armour plating was demonstrated startlingly when the magazines of the *Indefatigable* and the *Queen Mary* blew up leaving huge palls of smoke to mark the deaths of thousands of British sailors. Despite these British disasters, Hipper's ships were also hard hit.

The cruiser *Southampton* signalled Beatty shortly after 4.30 p.m. warning of the approach of Scheer with the main battle fleet from the SE, closing the trap on the British forces. Beatty turned away to fall back on Jellicoe hoping the enemy would follow course. During this run to the north the battle-cruisers clashed again and

Hipper's flagship *Lützow* was badly damaged. Beatty joined Jellicoe and at about 6 p.m. action between the main battle fleets appeared imminent.

Jellicoe manœuvred his fleet to cross the enemy's T and cut off his line of retreat while Scheer was unaware of Jellicoe's proximity. But the British suffered further losses: two armoured cruisers were overwhelmed when the First Cruiser Squadron ran into the German battle fleet and shortly afterwards Rear Admiral Hood lost his flagship *Invincible*, blown up again by Hipper's brilliantly accurate gunfire.

By now the main battle fleets were engaged and Scheer described a remarkable about-turn, a masterpiece of fleet handling, extricating his fleet from grave danger under cover of smoke and diversionary destroyer attacks. So skilful was this manœuvre that Jellicoe was unaware of the move and the High Seas Fleet withdrew to the SW.

Just before 7 p.m. Scheer advanced to the attack again and the second main action followed. The German ships suffered heavy punishment in this phase but Scheer again extricated his fleet successfully. At 7.20 p.m. Jellicoe turned away to the SE fearing torpedo attacks and this allowed Scheer to continue withdrawing to the SE. This was crucial. Contact between the opposing battle-fleets was lost, never to be regained. Sporadic fighting continued till nightfall and a twenty minute duel between Beatty's and Hipper's ships ended before 9 p.m.

Jellicoe declined a night action and deployed his forces to intercept Scheer and his withdrawal on the following morning. By then Scheer had reached the safety of the Horn Reef Channel, Jellicoe realized the enemy had eluded him and the Grand Fleet returned to Scapa Flow to face bitter controversy and recrimination for failing to bring the High Seas Fleet to decisive action.

Prince Albert aboard the *Collingwood* passed the wreck of the *Invincible*, saw the cruisers *Defiance* and *Black Prince* disappear beneath palls of smoke and saw huge holes rent in the sides of the *Derfflinger*. He wrote of his experiences to King George:

We went to 'Action Stations' at 4.30 p.m. and saw the Battle Cruisers in action ahead of us on the starboard bow. Some of the

Opposite Top *Queen Victoria's Diamond Jubilee Naval Review at Spithead. This painting by Charles Dixon shows the royal yacht passing along a column of dreadnoughts dressed overall with flags and bunting. (National Maritime Museum).* Bottom *The glorious painted hall of the Royal Naval College at Greenwich, familiar to many royal admirals, was designed by Sir Christopher Wren and decorated by Sir James Thornhill. (Woodmansterne)*

other cruisers were firing on the port bow . . . As far as one could see only 2 German Battle Squadrons and all their Battle Cruisers were out. The *Colossus* leading the 6th division with the *Collingwood* her next astern were nearest the enemy . . . We opened fire at 5.37 p.m. on some German light cruisers. The *Collingwood*'s second salvo hit one of them which set her on fire, and sank after two more salvoes were fired into her. We then shifted onto another light cruiser and helped to sink her as well. Our next target was a battle cruiser, we think the *Derrflinger* [sic] or *Lützow*, and one of the *Collingwood*'s salvoes hit her abaft the after turret, which burst into a fierce flame. After this she turned away from us and disappeared into the mist. By this time it was too dark to fire . . . The Germans fired some of their torpedoes but only one of them took effect in the *Marlborough*, the flagship of the 1st Battle Squadron . . . One torpedo passed ahead of the *Collingwood* and another astern. We had no casualties and no damage done to us, though we were 'straddled' several times . . .

I was in A turret and watched most of the action through one of the trainer's telescopes as we were firing by Director . . . At the commencement I was sitting on top of A turret and had a good view of the proceedings. I was up there during a lull when a German ship started firing at us, and one salvo 'straddled' us . . . I was distinctly startled and jumped down the hole in the top of the turret like a shot rabbit!!

Bertie's participation in the battle had a psychological effect upon him: it had brought him a new experience; the excitement of battle; the thrill of danger; the relief of survival; the comradeship of shared experience; and the pride of service.

'Bertie is very proud at having been in action', King George wrote later, 'but is sorry that his ship was not hit . . . as she had nothing to show she had been in a fight.'

Three months later Prince Albert was laid low again by acute stomach pains. He was sent ashore, a duodenal ulcer was diagnosed and, had he but known it, his *Collingwood* days were over. Before he took up his next appointment he survived a dangerous experience aboard a new steam driven submarine, the *K 3*. Bertie wrote to his father: 'We went out into the Solent and dived. It was rather

Opposite *Sir John Lavery's splendid painting shows King George V as an Admiral of the Fleet and Prince Edward as a midshipman with Queen Mary and the Princess Royal. (National Portrait Gallery)*

Prince Albert is shown here as a lieutenant in 1917. (Her Majesty the Queen)

an unfortunate dive as we stuck her nose in the mud for a quarter of an hour. Her crew were quite new, and they had forgotten to flood one of the forward tanks when they flooded the remainder. So when they did flood it, her bows went down very fast into the mud. It was not serious and they soon blew the water out again. It was most interesting and a great experience.'

On 8 May 1917 Prince Albert joined the 27,500 ton battleship *Malaya*, Captain the Hon. Algernon Boyle, with the rank of Acting Lieutenant. His wardroom shipmates proved to be a vintage lot, no less than eight of them later achieving flag rank—four of them C-in-Cs and two Admirals of the Fleet.

But, sadly, Bertie's days in the navy were numbered. Further gastric attacks developed and despite some months' recuperation in North Wales, Prince Albert himself came to the unhappy conclusion—despite his love for the navy—that he was constitutionally unfit for continued service at sea. His parents agreed and in November 1917 he underwent another operation and, successful though it was, it terminated his naval seagoing career of three years and eleven months. But a tenuous link with the navy was retained, for on recovering his health Bertie was transferred to the Royal Naval Air Service, joining the 'stone frigate' HMS *Daedalus* in February 1918, that collection of hutments and hangars on the windswept plateau at Cranwell in Lincolnshire where pilots and air gunners were trained for aeroplanes and dirigibles. In due course the RNAS was incorporated into a unified Royal Air Force which came into existence on 1 April 1918 so even this tenuous naval link was broken.

Prince Albert never resumed active service but he received

regular promotions, to Commander at the end of 1920, to Captain five years later, to Rear Admiral in 1932 and Vice Admiral in 1936. In December 1936 when Bertie's brother Edward VIII abdicated, Albert inherited the throne to which task he brought the high sense of duty learned from his father and from the navy to restore prestige to the Crown—and at that time he assumed the rank of Admiral of the Fleet.

Prince Albert's younger brother—Prince George Edward Alexander Edmund, fourth son of King George V—followed in Prince Edward's and Albert's wake into the Royal Navy, although he is chiefly remembered for his devotion to the Royal Air Force and his death on active service in the RAF. As a youngster he had been spared the isolation of private tuition under the ineffectual Mr Hansell and together with brother Henry, later the Duke of Gloucester, he attended a fashionable preparatory school in Broadstairs. He passed the qualifying examination for the navy and entered the RN College at Osborne, enrolling in the Starboard watch of the Hawke Term. But like Albert and Edward before him he achieved deplorably low term positions in his examinations. He fared little better at Dartmouth and Prince Albert was impelled to write to a friend in May 1920 when George left for a training cruise in the 18,600 ton Dreadnought battleship, veteran of Jutland, the *Temeraire*: 'He has kept up the best traditions of my family by passing out of Dartmouth 1 from bottom, the same place as I did!!!!'

George's cheerful nature attracted many friends and his natural charm, piano playing ability and liking for sport more than compensated for his lack of academic achievement.

His 1920 training cruise took him to Oslo, Vigo, Gibraltar, Algiers, Malta, Palma and Lisbon, a cruise lasting about eight months which endeared him to the navy and his chosen career.

In January of the new year Prince George was awarded his midshipman's tabs and with sixteen colleagues was appointed to the Mediterranean, to the C-in-C's flagship, none other than the 25,000-ton battleship *Iron Duke*, flagship of Admiral Sir John Jellicoe at Jutland in 1916 and remembered by many sailors of World War II as an ignominious depot ship at Scapa Flow.

Prince George is shown here as a sub-lieutenant in 1924. (Her Majesty the Queen)

A year after George joined the ship, the C-in-C, Admiral Sir John de Robeck, transferred his flag to his new flagship of the Atlantic Fleet, the majestic 27,500-ton battleship *Queen Elizabeth*, with her massive eight 15-inch guns. Midshipman Prince George joined the gunroom as senior midshipman.

Some small ship training was undertaken in the 1800-ton destroyer *Mackay* then illness struck and George, like brother Bertie, was operated on for appendicitis. Months of sick leave followed before his career was resumed with courses at Portsmouth and the RN College, Greenwich.

After promotion to Sub-Lieutenant in January 1924 George was appointed to the 9750-ton light cruiser HMS *Hawkins*, flagship of Vice Admiral Sir Allan Everett, C-in-C of the China Station, who was soon to be relieved by Admiral Sir Edwin Alexander-Sinclair, the commanding officer of Osborne College during Prince Edward's cadetship. A good deal of the *Hawkins*'s commission was spent as guardship in the muddy waters of the Whangpoo at Shanghai, then the teeming international settlement, but cruises took the ship to Hong Kong, Penang and Port Swettenham. Prince George spent some months on secondment to the gunboat HMS *Bee* and experienced the thrills and dangers of patrol work with the Yangtse Flotilla.

In February 1926 he was promoted to Lieutenant and on return home spent four months on a study course in France to qualify as an interpreter in French. In the following year he was appointed to the staff of Vice Admiral Sir Hubert Brand, commanding the Atlantic Fleet with his flag in the new 33,950-ton battleship *Nelson*. This was a prestigious appointment for a young officer but it was marred for Prince George by the recurrent bouts of stomach upsets which necessitated spells of sick leave.

In the summer of 1928 George joined the light cruiser *Durban*, a vessel of only 4850 tons, as junior lieutenant before the ship sailed for her new station based on Bermuda, the most treasured posting by sailors for the show-the-flag cruises took in many of the tropical ports of the West Indies and South America.

Prince George enjoyed several months in an extensive cruise down to the broad, calm waters of the estuary of the River Plate to Montevideo and elegant Buenos Aires, then south round the Horn through less hospitable waters to Valparaiso in Chile and further north to Peru's Callao. At every port of call demands were made upon the royal sailor's time to undertake official visits, to officiate at ceremonies and functions which George found exhausting and it became increasingly evident to him that despite nearly ten years' service in the navy he was finding his constitution—like brother Bertie's—too weak for continuous sea-time. In consequence, in 1929 on return from the West Indies Prince George retired from active naval service.

He received promotion to Commander in February 1934, the year of his marriage in November to Princess Marina, daughter of Prince Nicholas of Greece, an event which gave George a new sense of purpose in life. Shortly before the wedding he had been created Duke of Kent. In January 1937 he was promoted to Captain and to Rear Admiral in June 1939 just months before the outbreak of World War II. It was in that rank that he was appointed as Staff Officer (Intelligence) to the C-in-C at Rosyth on the outbreak of war. But it was to the RAF that George turned to give service to his country and it was on 25 August 1942 as an Air Commodore that he embarked aboard a Sunderland flying boat of Coastal Command to fly from Cromarty Firth to Iceland. The aircraft crashed in foul weather near the village of Dunbeath and HRH the Duke of Kent, royal admiral extraordinary, first royal prince to have flown the Atlantic, was also the first to die in an air disaster—at the age of forty.

9

Earl Mountbatten of Burma

HIS SERENE HIGHNESS Prince Louis Francis Victor Nicholas of Battenberg was born on 25 June 1900 at Frogmore House, Windsor. The youngest child of Admiral Louis of Battenberg and Princess Victoria, in the style of most members of the royal families of Europe, was given a totally different name by the family: to intimates and friends he was known as Dickie all his life.

Dickie's lineage was a royal and illustrious one encompassing more than one thousand years of history, traceable from Charlemagne himself—Charles the Great, Emperor of the Holy Roman Empire—to the great Queen Victoria, Empress of the greatest modern empire.

Another of Dickie's ancestors with estates in Lorraine and Brabant inherited the principality of Hesse in the thirteenth century and in 1529 Philip of Hesse gave the world the new word Protestant, derived from the Protest which he helped compose. Numbered among Dickie's other relations were dukes and grand dukes, princes and tsars; he was linked to all the royal houses of Europe: it was a majestic family into which he had been born, yet this obstreperous baby was destined to match, if not outshine them all.

Dickie's interest in the navy stemmed initially from his father who was a captain at the time of the baby's birth and was soon to reach flag rank and the highest offices of the navy—but also from older brother Georgie, eight years his senior, whom he adored and who entered the Royal Naval College at Osborne in 1905 and took every opportunity to wear his cadet's uniform which he wore with pride.

Dickie entered the Royal Naval College at Osborne as a cadet on

8 May 1913, a few weeks before his thirteenth birthday, having had the benefit of a preparatory school education, unlike his contemporaries, the Windsor princes. He entered the navy at a significant period of its development. Winston Churchill at the Admiralty had appointed Prince Louis, Dickie's father, to the highest professional post in the navy—First Sea Lord; strategy was agreed to combat the menace of a re-arming Germany; the adoption of a distant blockade of Germany was planned; a Naval War Staff had been created; naval bases at Cromarty, Rosyth and Scapa Flow were re-developed. Churchill, in characteristic manner, muddied the naval and political waters, upsetting many traditionalists; in eighteen months of office at the Admiralty he spent 182 days at sea, an unprecedented record for a First Lord. Dickie's mother had thought Churchill unreliable because he had once borrowed a book and failed to return it. This unreliability was confirmed by Dickie

Cadet Dickie photographed outside the official London residence of the First Sea Lord, his father Prince Louis Battenberg, in 1913. (Broadlands Archives)

when Churchill visited Osborne College and asked the cadets if there were any complaints. Only Dickie had the audacity to say could he get the cadets three sardines for Sunday supper instead of two! When the three were not forthcoming, Dickie's doubts about Churchill were confirmed.

A major development in Dickie's Osborne phase came in 1914 when, as we have already read, Prince Louis and Churchill mobilized the fleet, including the Reservists and to the cadets' excitement they were also mobilized and Dickie found himself sent to the battleship *New Zealand*—brother Georgie's ship.

The Royal Review of the Fleet at Spithead followed the Test

Mobilization and the experience made a lasting impression on Dickie. 59 battleships, 24 of them Dreadnoughts, 55 cruisers, 78 destroyers and an armada of smaller ships assembled in powerful testimony to the efforts of Fisher, Churchill, Battenberg and their policies.

It took more than six hours for this armada to pass before the royal yacht at 15 knots, every ship decked with flags and crowded with sailors and marines.

Dickie and Georgie survived the shock of their father's resignation as First Sea Lord and Dickie went on to complete his Dartmouth training, coming through the final examinations very creditably indeed. His first sea-going appointment was to HMS *Lion*, the flagship of Admiral Sir David Beatty, then undergoing repairs only seven weeks after the Battle of Jutland.

Beatty was a hero to every midshipman, not least to the sixteen-year-old Dickie, and to join the hero's battle-scarred flagship was unbelievable luck. The well-known anecdote about Beatty at Jutland was on every midshipman's lips. At the height of the battle with two of his battle-cruisers blown up and with his own flagship afire, Beatty turned to his flag captain and remarked, 'There's something wrong with our bloody ships today, Chatfield. Turn two points to port'—i.e. nearer to the enemy.

Dickie considered his brother Georgie to have been incredibly lucky for not only did he fight as a gunnery lieutenant aboard the *New Zealand* at the Battle of Jutland but at Heligoland Bight and the Dogger Bank as well. Indeed, it has been calculated that in these battles the 12-inch guns of Prince George's turret fired more rounds than any other turret of any battleship, German or British. Georgie was thought by many to have been quite brilliant. Dickie related the story about Georgie: 'He could lie on his back in the ward-room, talk and laugh on a hundred subjects and then—looking at his watch—dictate a Draft for the Fleet Gunnery Orders, which, without correction or revision, would not only be issued but kept afterwards as an example of lucidity!'*

Life for the young midshipmen was tough and tiring; sleeping in hammocks, scrubbing out the gunroom, watch-keeping by day,

---

* *Last Viceroy*, Ray Murphy, Jarrolds Publishers, n.d.

The Queen Elizabeth *is shown here during the Gallipoli campaign. This water-colour is by Charles Dixon. (National Maritime Museum)*

running a picket boat, enduring all the traditional indignities of being a gunroom snotty and the most anguishing chore of all—coaling ship. Coal had to be shovelled from the hold of a collier alongside, bagged, transported aboard the battle-cruiser and distributed along the holds. Everyone took part, officers included, and all endured the gritty, exhausting experience time after time.

But such ordeals did nothing to diminish Dickie's love for his naval life to which he devoted all his energies and even at this early phase of his career he was showing a strong determination to learn and to lead. When his great hero transferred his flag to the battleship *Queen Elizabeth* as C-in-C of the Grand Fleet, Dickie was proud to join the flagship also.

As the war dragged on through its third year with the mounting horrors of carnage on the Western Front, unrestricted U-boat warfare, published casualty lists making sombre reading, Zeppelin raids, conscription of men and mobilization of women; an embittered nation—public opinion, no less—impelled King George to proclaim a change of family name to Windsor; Queen Mary's family name of Teck was to become Cambridge and the Battenberg family name changed to Mountbatten. Prince Louis was granted the title of Marquess of Milford Haven, Earl of Medina and Viscount Alderney. Georgie assumed his father's second title until he inherited the marquessate and Dickie became Lord Louis Mountbatten.

Much worse than mere name changing was to befall Mountbatten's close Russian relations for whom he held great affection. Fierce ordeals were to overtake the Tsar: in the first Russian Revolution of 1917 he abdicated and with his family was kept under house arrest at Tsarskoe Selo. Later, they were brutally murdered. Mountbatten's cousin, the fourteen-year-old haemophilic Tsarevitch, heir to the throne, needed three more bullets to kill him and the young and beautiful Anastasia (despite persistent reports of her survival) was bayonetted to death. When the news reached England the English court and the Mountbattens were shocked and dismayed. Mountbatten recalled that the four young grand duchesses seemed to get more attractive every time he saw them

Dickie Mountbatten's aunt, the Tsarina of Russia, the Tsar (Battenberg's cousin), the Tsarevitch, and the four Grand Duchesses: Anastasia, Marie, Olga and Tatiana. (Broadlands Archives)

and he often declared later that he secretly hoped to marry Marie.

A few months before the November armistice in 1918, after five years' naval training and apprenticeship, Mountbatten was promoted Sub-Lieutenant and appointed as Second-in-Command of the small anti-submarine vessel *P 31* attached to the Portsmouth Escort Flotilla, a year-long experience in small ships quickly followed by a two-term stint at Christ's College, Cambridge, part of an Admiralty scheme for the further education of young officers.

In July 1920 Mountbatten strengthened his friendship with his cousin, the Prince of Wales, when he was invited to become Flag Lieutenant to Rear Admiral Sir Lionel Halsey, Chief of Staff to the Prince aboard HMS *Renown* on a tour of New Zealand, Australia and the West Indies. It was a dazzling prospect for the twenty-two-year-old Mountbatten to accompany his cousin—heir apparent to the world's greatest crown. Mountbatten was also pleased by the thought that the commanding officer of the *Renown* was Captain the Hon. Herbert Meade, a son of the Earl of Clanwilliam who had commanded the Flying Squadron in which Mountbatten's father had served in 1880.

The tour had its lighter moments and on Crossing the Line both the Prince and Mountbatten were subjected to all the indignities of a Royal Navy version of the traditional ritual of King Neptune coming aboard accompanied by Queen Amphitrite, bodyguards, the Chief Herald, the Chief Bear, Judges, three Barbers and sundry assistants. All novices—including the two royal sailors—were thoroughly lathered in black, purple and white then shaved before being tilted backwards into the bath to be ducked viciously by the Bears. It was a light-hearted but alarming experience.

More alarming was the experience of a rail accident which the royal party suffered during the visit of nearly three months to Australia when every state and capital was visited. In Western Australia the eight-coach train suffered a series of jolts before the last two coaches containing the royal party and the ministerial staffs left the rails and overturned with a violent, grinding crash. All the royal party escaped injury but it had been a miraculous escape. Fortunately the train had not been travelling fast because of a cow obstructing the line: the Prince of Wales later declared the cow deserved the MVO. When the royal party came to examine the track the rails were torn and twisted for eighty yards behind the royal coach and marks indicated that the coaches had been off the rails for another 230 yards further still.

The *Renown* returned to Portsmouth via the Panama Canal in October 1920 and it was soon after this and the distressing death of his father that Mountbatten met a debutante named Edwina Cynthia Annette Ashley. Before he could bestow much attention on Edwina, Mountbatten departed with the Prince of Wales on the next grand tour, that of 1920-1 when India, Burma, Ceylon, Malaya and Japan were visited.

In India the opulence, splendour, lavish banquets and magnificence of the Maharajahs and Nawabs was a glittering experience but it marked the underlying tragedy of this great nation and its poverty and starvation. Evidence of the growing swell of nationalistic opposition to British rule even at that time was given by Mahatma Gandhi who demonstrated in favour of a boycott of the royal tour in Bombay.

It was in India that Mountbatten took up polo which was to become a passion with him. In a TV appearance in 1967 he declared that in India he found three loves: 'The first of these was India herself. Staying with the princes I found my second love—polo . . . and finally my real love . . .'

Edwina Ashley was the grand-daughter of Sir Ernest Cassel, an intimate friend of Edward VII (who was Edwina's godfather), and a wealthy banker and financier: he financed the Mexican railways, negotiated loans for China, aided the finances of Argentina, assisted the Swedish railway system, and financed Egypt's greatest dam project. He was a man of immense presence, owner of splendid houses, expensively and ornately furnished with classical furniture and paintings by the great masters. Most of this wealth was to be Edwina's inheritance. One such home was Brook House in exclusive Park Lane overlooking Hyde Park. Many years later on the death of her father, Lord Mount Temple (the one-time Colonel Wilfred Ashley and husband of Cassel's daughter) Edwina inherited the superb estate of Broadlands with its eighteenth-century palladian façade. On the walls of this beautiful home hung portraits by Reynolds, Lely, Van Dyck. Through the extensive park of the estate with its orangery, trimmed hedges and gardens flows the

The wedding of Lord Louis Mountbatten and Edwina Ashley. The Prince of Wales was best man. The bridesmaids were the four sisters of Prince Philip, the Princesses Margarita, Theodora, Cecile and Sophie; the bride's sister, Mary Ashley; her cousin, Joan Pakenham and Lady Mary Ashley-Cooper. (Broadlands Archives)

River Test, one of England's most famous dry-fly trout streams.

Royal consent was needed for the marriage; this was the result of the Duke of Cumberland's churlish behaviour one hundred and fifty years before; consent was readily forthcoming but the Vicereine of India, Lady Reading, wrote to Edwina's aunt about her reservations: 'I hoped she would have cared for someone older, with more of a career before him.'

The marriage of Lord Louis Mountbatten and Edwina Ashley brought together the brilliance of the Battenberg lineage and the wealth of the Cassel banking empire. It was a most propitious liaison. The wedding was the naval and social event of the year with King George, Queen Mary and Queen Alexandra attending and the Prince of Wales acting as best man. The honeymoon in Europe was extended by an understanding Admiralty and the couple visited the USA—Washington, Florida, Los Angeles, Hollywood—where they stayed at the Fairbanks' home 'Pickfair' in Beverley Hills— New York, Chicago and Niagara Falls. They met President Harding, Jerome Kern, Babe Ruth and Charlie Chaplin.

In January 1923 Lieutenant Mountbatten returned to his naval duties aboard the battleship HMS *Revenge* lying at Constantinople and soon afterwards he took the decision to specialize in the signals branch. At the end of the year he joined the Signal School at Portsmouth and went on to the Higher Wireless Course at Greenwich. He had made a wise choice. Communications became a vocation and in 1927 Mountbatten, now a Lieutenant-Commander, was given the prestigious appointment of Fleet Wireless Officer of the Mediterranean Fleet aboard the flagship HMS *Queen Elizabeth*. The C-in-C was the naval hero of Zeebrugge, Admiral Sir Roger Keyes who later admitted to Mountbatten that he had vetoed the appointment: 'I didn't want a cousin of the King out here on my staff.' But he relented on remembering the support he had been given as a young officer by Prince Battenberg, so he telegraphed the Admiralty accepting the appointment.

Although Mountbatten enjoyed a popularity among his colleagues in the navy he also aroused feelings of resentment and even prejudice for his ostentation, for his intensity, for a hint of vulgarity in his easy superiority, the product of his utter professionalism. He was even black-balled from the exclusive Royal Yacht Squadron some of whose members thought he might introduce an undesirable element into the club. Later, the snub was overruled and Mountbatten was persuaded to accept an invitation to join.

Mountbatten was later to recall these years in the Mediterranean as heady days: he was excelling in his career, acknowledged to be an expert in wireless telegraphy, he was revelling in the skills and thrills of polo, showing-the-flag cruises, weekend picnics and he enjoyed having Edwina and their first child, Patricia, living with him at their charming house called Casa Medina.

In 1928 he transferred to the destroyer flotilla leader *Stuart*, later to earn renown as an old veteran destroyer in the Mediterranean in World War II, as Staff Signals Officer to Captain (D). In the following year when the flotilla was visiting Barcelona, another daughter, Pamela, was born to the Mountbattens. Edwina drove to meet her

husband at a Barcelona hotel and the bumpy ride probably accelerated the arrival of the baby. Mountbatten searched high and low
for assistance but the only doctor in the hotel was an elderly throat
specialist. As a last resort he telephoned his cousin Queen Ena in
Madrid for advice, but she was away and the call was put through
to the King, Alfonso. He was much excited by the news but the
action he took served no useful purpose: the bemedalled Military
Governor of Barcelona—commanded by the King—turned out
with officers and soldiers to guard the hotel. If anything, they served
only to delay matters and add to the confusion. In due course a
suitable doctor arrived—and so did Pamela.

The family returned to England to allow Mountbatten to take up
his appointment as Senior Instructor in Wireless Telegraphy at
Portsmouth Signal School to which task he brought his reforming
zeal and contagious enthusiasm. But this two-year spell of duty was
merely an interruption to his days in the Mediterranean. He returned to Malta in 1931 as Fleet Wireless Officer responsible for
radio communications throughout the seventy ships of the fleet and
one of his major achievements during this time was the part he and
the navy took in the inauguration of the Empire Broadcasting
Service with the first Christmas Day broadcast by King George V
in 1932. The C-in-C ordered the Fleet Wireless Officer to ensure
that everyone in the services and all civilians ashore in Malta should
hear the King's voice. In a few hectic weeks Mountbatten and all
communications officers and ratings in the fleet laboured hard and
long to perform the technical mysteries of receiving and relaying
the broadcast. Receivers were installed in hospitals, shops, street
corners, public squares and inside cinemas. Transmitters, a new
H/F receiver and masses of other equipment had to be adapted and
set up for the occasion. The last components arrived as late as
Christmas Eve, but all went well and the broadcast was received
clearly throughout the island and the fleet.

On promotion to Commander—Mountbatten's career was proceeding along conventional lines—he attended a course at the
Naval Tactical School before enjoying the thrill of his first command. The year was 1934; the undertones of war were faintly stir-
ring in Europe and many new ships were coming off the British
stocks. HMS *Daring* was one such ship—a destroyer—and it fell

to Mountbatten's good fortune to have her given as his first command. He experienced the exhilaration felt by his royal predecessors—Prince Alfred, his cousin Prince George and his father Prince Louis. Mountbatten's star was still in the ascendant, but it dimmed, at least temporarily when his flotilla was ordered to Singapore to swop destroyers with the China Destroyer Flotilla: in the exchange Mountbatten was given command of a much inferior ship, an old Thorneycroft Modified 'W' Class destroyer, the *Wishart*, laid down in 1919 and displacing 1140 tons.

Mountbatten liked recalling his addressing the ship's company; typically, he searched around for a novel way of capturing the men's imagination:

We have just left a ship with a great name—the *Daring*—a wonderful name. We have come to the only ship in the navy with a greater name. For our ship is called after the Almighty himself, to whom we pray every day: 'Our Father Wishart in Heaven'.

It was a brave effort.

On his return to the Mediterranean Mountbatten audaciously set about making his ageing destroyer Cock of the Fleet. His driving spirit enthused his ship's company to high levels of attainment with the result that the *Wishart* carried off practically every regatta trophy, including those for cricket and water-polo plus the more technically specialized naval skills of gunnery and communications. No sooner had Mountbatten worked up his crew to a high pitch of efficiency than he was appointed to the Naval Air Division of the Admiralty.

Thus, at a specially interesting period of naval history, a long period of preparation for war, of emergence from appeasement and finally mobilization of the navy at the time of Munich, Mountbatten was at the very centre of gravity of decision-making, and, indeed, contributing to the making of some of these decisions— such as the introduction of the Oerlikon gun into the Royal Navy.

When an expatriate Austrian engineer named Antoine Gazda, working for the Swiss Oerlikon works visited London to make an exclusive offer to the British Government of a revolutionary new AA weapon he was shunted off to Mountbatten. When Gazda revealed that the weapon's rate of fire was about five hundred HE 20 shells per minute with a muzzle velocity roughly twice that of any other gun of its weight, Mountbatten was impressed and recognized the importance of the weapon. He threw all his weight into this project and this meeting he had with Gazda was to be the first of no less than 283 between the Admiralty and Gazda in the ensuing years before the Oerlikon was finally adopted as an effective defence weapon for warships and merchantmen against enemy dive-bombers. Thousands were subsequently fitted to British and US ships during World War II.

Another air problem of greater political significance, the transference back to the navy of control of the Fleet Air Arm, also called for much strenuous work by Mountbatten.

It was during Mountbatten's tour of duty at the Admiralty that King George V—the Sailor King—died and bequeathed the crown to Edward, Prince of Wales, Mountbatten's best friend and cousin, who now became King Edward VIII. The reign set off with high expectations, a modern monarchy replacing the rather severe image of King George. But the event which became known as the Abdication Crisis aroused the nation with feelings of great emotion. The new king openly expressed to Prime Minister Mr Stanley Baldwin his wish to marry Mrs Wallis Simpson but Baldwin resolutely refused to accommodate the King on the grounds that as a divorced woman Mrs Simpson could not be married in the Church of England nor could she be crowned Queen and Baldwin's steadfast stance brought on the Abdication of 10 December 1936.

Prince Albert—Bertie—ill-prepared for the burden he was now asked to shoulder was encouraged by Mountbatten's quoting Prince Battenberg's words to King George V that naval training was the best preparation for being a king. Albert, the reluctant King George VI, was to prove this point and, in doing so, was to win the affection of the nation in the ordeals that lay ahead.

From the Higher Commanders Course at Aldershot which followed Mountbatten's Admiralty appointment, he was given command of the 5th Destroyer Flotilla of brand new ships with HMS *Kelly* as leader. He took her over from Hawthorn Leslie ten days before the outbreak of war in 1939 and entered upon a phase of his life which captured the public imagination more even than his

The famous Kelly, *leader of the 5th Destroyer Flotilla, of which Lord Louis Mountbatten became Captain in 1939. (Imperial War Museum)*

periods as Viceroy of India or Supremo in South-East Asia Command. The destroyer *Kelly* and her thrilling exploits with the dashing, handsome, royal sailor on the bridge won the admiration of a nation wearied by defeat after defeat: Mountbatten's friend Noel Coward translated the *Kelly*'s exploits into the film *In Which We Serve*—with much artistic licence—in a tribute not only to *Kelly* and her captain but to the Royal Navy as a whole.

Kelly's was an exciting but brief career of twenty-one months. One of her first duties was to collect the Duke and Duchess of Windsor from exile in France to return to England. Shortly afterwards the *Kelly* was struck well aft by a mine in the North Sea but survived the experience only to suffer torpedoing in the Norwegian campaign during the disastrous spring of 1940. The torpedoing was witnessed by Mountbatten's nephew Lord Milford Haven in the destroyer next astern—the *Kandahar*; so great was the explosion that it was thought there could be no survivors. But the ship did not sink. The destroyer *Bulldog* got a tow aboard. The *Kelly* was so low in the water that her starboard gunwale was awash and in order to give her a chance of survival Mountbatten jettisoned all the topweight possible: ten torpedoes were fired off, depth

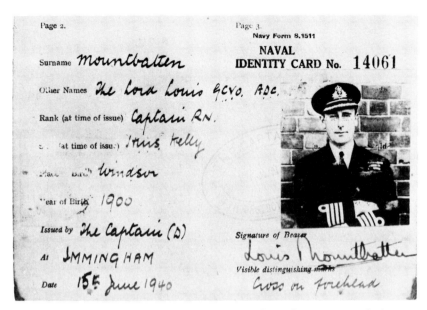

Navy Form S.1511

NAVAL
IDENTITY CARD No. 14061

Surname *Mountbatten*

Other Names *The Lord Louis GCVO, ADC.*

Rank (at time of issue) *Captain RN.*

... (at time of issue) *HMS Kelly*

Place birth *Windsor*

Year of Birth *1900*

Issued by *The Captain (D)*

At *IMMINGHAM*

Date *15th June 1940*

Signature of Bearer

Louis Mountbatten

Visible distinguishing marks

Cross on forehead

During the war royal sailors too had to comply with service regulations and carry their naval identity cards. This one was issued to Lord Louis Mountbatten while he was Captain of the Kelly. *(Broadlands Archives)*

---

charges ditched and lockers, boats and ammunition cast over the side. All but six officers and twelve men were transferred to further reduce topweight.

During the first night of the tow an MTB, thought to have been an enemy E-boat, stormed on to the scene, guns firing, collided— it was only a glancing blow—with the *Bulldog*, actually came aboard the *Kelly*'s starboard side and carried away davits and guardrails as she passed down the destroyer's side. It was an unbelievable experience. After three and a half days of towing the *Kelly* came home to Hebburn to a Tyneside welcome.

While the *Kelly* was being repaired Mountbatten continued to command the flotilla from the *Javelin* but she, too, was torpedoed by a salvo which struck her in the bows and the stern. She also managed to survive the tow to Devonport.

Kelly's end came in the Mediterranean during the fierce ordeals of the naval battles in the dangerous waters off Crete. It was a time when over-worked ships of the Royal Navy with exhausted crews contested control of the Cretan waters with the Luftwaffe and suffered crippling losses at the hands of the Stuka pilots. After a disastrous campaign in Greece resulting in the evacuation of

British troops, the island of Crete fell to the German parachute battalions. In the last phase of the battle the Royal Navy was called upon to mount yet another rescue under intense aerial bombardment.

On 22 May 1941 the *Kelly*, in company with *Kashmir*, was sailing from Crete, recalled to Alexandria. Just before 8 a.m. on 23 May, twenty-four Ju 87 Stukas located the fleeing ships and launched determined attacks, so determined that they dived almost vertically ensuring great accuracy of bombing and offering the minimal silhouette for gunners manning the 4.7-inch, Oerlikon and pom-pom guns.

The *Kashmir* was struck by a 500-kg bomb from an aircraft of the third wave of bombers which caused enormous damage and she soon began to sink. Her commanding officer, Commander H. A. King, ordered abandon ship and she sank in two minutes.

The full bombardment was now directed against the *Kelly*. She fought back ferociously but was hit by a large bomb which exploded aft on her X turret while she was making 30 knots and under full starboard rudder. She took on an ever-increasing list to port, aided by the full rudder and finally turned turtle with considerable way on her. She floated upside down for half an hour allowing her survivors to get well clear before she finally sank.

Kipling, commanded by Commander A. St Clair-Ford, was not far away from the battle scene and sped to rescue survivors. Mountbatten and King were among those clutched from the sea but the *Kelly* lost one hundred and thirty men and the *Kashmir* eighty-two. Throughout the rescue attempts the *Kipling* was subjected to bombing attacks by Ju 88s: as each attack developed the *Kipling* abandoned the rescue, put on speed and dodged the bombs while fighting off the assailants. This tactic led to a tragic incident. The ship's motor boat was still secured to the falls when St Clair-Ford got the destroyer under way rapidly. There was no time to release the boat. It dragged under, tearing the davits from the destroyer's deck and carried to their deaths the First Lieutenant of the *Kipling*, Lieut.-Commander J. E. A. Bush and the First Lieutenant of the *Kelly*, Lieut.-Commander Lord Hugh Beresford, both of whom were trying to cut the falls.

After three hours of nosing from raft to raft pulling survivors

HMS Kipling *arriving in Alexandria to the cheers of the fleet.*
(Imperial War Museum)

aboard and dodging attacks, *Kipling* was left in peace. She had withstood over eighty bombs—yet escaped unscathed. Even before reaching sanctuary, the *Kipling* was to run out of fuel some miles from Alexandria before being refuelled and arriving to a hero's welcome. Hers was an epic of survival but the lesson was not lost to Mountbatten and other more senior officers: she was the sole survivor of three modern, well-armed, high-speed destroyers, competently handled with plenty of sea room in combat with dive bombers. General Richthoven wrote in his War Diary at the time: 'We had at last demonstrated that a fleet at sea within range of the Luftwaffe was vulnerable . . .'

Almost the first person Mountbatten met when he stepped ashore was his nephew Prince Philip, a midshipman then serving aboard the *Valiant*, who teased his uncle about his grimy appearance.

With the loss of the *Kelly*, Mountbatten entered a new phase of his life for he was selected by the Prime Minister for higher things than command of a ship at sea. Mountbatten was recalled from the USA where he had gone to join the aircraft carrier *Illustrious* then refitting in Norfolk after bomb damage in a Malta convoy. At Chequers, Churchill told Mountbatten that he was to be Adviser on Combined Operations—to which the Captain replied he would rather be back at sea in command. The Prime Minister was visibly irritated. 'Have you no sense of glory? Here I give you the chance to take a part in the higher leadership of the war and all you want to do is to go back to sea! What can you hope to achieve except to be sunk in a bigger and more expensive ship?'

Churchill was right, as Mountbatten quickly appreciated. Mountbatten, the young—and some thought, brash—naval captain was to replace the elderly and respected Admiral of the Fleet Sir Roger Keyes of Dardenelles and Zeebrugge fame on whose staff Mountbatten had served as a lieutenant in 1927. He took up his new appointment in October 1941 with the acting rank of Commodore. The prime duties in the new appointment were twofold: firstly, to continue the commando raids on the Continent and secondly, to prepare for the invasion of France—the so-called Second Front.

It was a post hedged about by political considerations, by interservice rivalry, by the innate distrust of someone trying to run a private army such as he appeared to be doing. He sat in on Chiefs of Staff meetings when Combined Operations were on the agenda. Only when, some months later, he became a member of the Chiefs of Staff committee in his own right was he enabled to exercise full authority in his post and his combined operations successes, the fathering of D-Day, stem from that membership. 'I want you', Churchill had ordered with Churchillian splendour 'to turn the south coast of England from a bastion of defence into a springboard for attack.'

Soon after Pearl Harbour had erupted on to a startled world in December 1941 the first of the commando raids was carried out against installations in the Lofoten and other Norwegian off-shore islands. In February 1942 a specially daring raid against the German radar station at Bruneval on the Cherbourg peninsula was executed with great success.

In the following month Mountbatten was given the acting rank of Vice Admiral at the age of forty-one, and for the first time ever for a serving officer, he was given honorary ranks of Lieutenant-

General and Air Marshal, and his title changed to Chief of Combined Operations.

That same month was marked by the combined operations raid on St Nazaire to smash the massive gates of the dry dock, the only dock on the Atlantic coast capable of housing the battleship *Tirpitz*. The old destroyer *Campbelltown* was sacrificed to ram the dock gates with her bows filled with high explosives and delayed action fuses. The raid was a complete success and was marked by incidents of great personal bravery. No less than five VCs were won on this day at St Nazaire.

Combined operations suffered its greatest defeat in the attack on Dieppe in August 1942 when six hundred Canadian and British troops landed in the face of fierce opposition in an essential rehearsal for the D-Day landings of two years later. Casualties were fearfully high but the hard lessons to be learned helped save countless thousands of lives during the mass invasion of the Normandy beaches later.

These operations and his duties as Chief of Combined Operations brought Mountbatten increasingly into the political arena and into the realms of international discussions, especially with the Americans. One of the first friendships he cemented was with General George Marshall, Chief of Staff of the US Army, and following Marshall's visit to England it was arranged that US Rangers would train with British Commandos in Scotland. During the planning and execution of Operation Torch—the invasion of North Africa in November 1942—and the assault on Sicily in July 1943, Mountbatten worked closer still with Marshall, with Air Force General Arnold and even managed to charm the difficult Admiral King to provide a flag officer to study the Combined Operations organization. Mountbatten brought to his dealings with others and to his job in particular all the tact, originality of thought and prodigious energy needed to overcome difficulties in steamrolling his plans through. PLUTO, the pipe line under the ocean which conveyed fuel to Normandy, the man-made Mulberry Harbour at Arromanches, the design and fitting-out of landing ships, and more importantly headquarters ships for landing craft like HMS *Bulolo*—all of these were events of significance demanding time and toil.

Mountbatten was no longer responsible for Combined Operations when the invasion forces of the Allies crossed the Channel in June 1944. It was appropriate that a signal was sent to him:

> Today we visited the British and American Armies on the soil of France. We sailed through vast fleets of ships with landing craft of many types pouring more men, vehicles and stores ashore. We saw clearly the manœuvre in process of rapid development. We have shared our secrets in common and helped each other all we could. We wish to tell you in this moment in your arduous campaign that we realise that much of this remarkable technique and therefore the success of the venture has its origin in developments effected by you and your staff of Combined Operations. [Signed]

ARNOLD	KING
BROOKE	MARSHALL
CHURCHILL	SMUTS

It was a magnanimous gesture.

Mountbatten's new appointment had been put to him by Churchill as they strolled along the battlements overlooking the Heights of Abraham. Churchill offered him the job of Supreme Allied Commander South-East Asia. Once again he irritated the prime minister by asking for twenty-four hours before making a decision. He wanted this time to secure reassurance that the British and US Chiefs of Staff—and President Roosevelt—would approve the choice and give him full backing: on receipt of these assurances Mountbatten promptly accepted Churchill's offer.

The Supremo job was a monumental one for so young a commander. Mountbatten, now ranked a full Admiral, was still only forty-three, five years below the top of the Captains List.

He had as Deputy the irascible American Lieutenant-General Joseph Stilwell—the famous fighting Vinegar Joe—who was prejudiced against the British but allowed himself to be won over by

Mountbatten's tough stand against Generalissimo Chiang Kai-Shek.

Mountbatten in South-East Asia was one of four Supreme Allied Commanders in the Far East. Admiral Chester Nimitz (born 1885) maintained the offensive against the Japanese navy in the central Pacific. The legendary General MacArthur (born 1880), based in Australia, commanded the South-West Pacific. Chiang Kai-Shek (born 1887) commanded in China.

Mountbatten moved in illustrious military circles. Lord Wavell was Viceroy of India. General Auckinleck commanded the armies in India; General Sir William Slim commanded the 14th Army in Burma; Orde Wingate commanded the Chindits; US General Stratemeyer commanded the Allied Air Forces in Burma. The total land forces under his command mainly comprised Indian, British and Gurkhas, a great number of Americans, Chinese, East and West Africans, Burmese, Australians, a few Frenchmen and some Dutchmen. Mountbatten set about the task of welding all these differing elements into one cohesive command with his customary zeal.

The retreat from Burma was halted. The invasion of India was baulked. The re-entry into Burma was launched and only days before the recapture of Burma's capital, President Franklin Roosevelt died and the English-speaking nations mourned.

Mountbatten met President Harry S. Truman in July 1945: victory in Europe had been achieved and the Potsdam Conference held with Churchill, Truman and Stalin where decisions were taken which were of immense consequence for the world. It was here that Mountbatten and colleagues learnt for the first time of the advent of the atomic era. The devastation of Nagasaki and Hiroshima brought the Japanese war to a rapid end and Mountbatten accepted the surrender of 680,879 Japanese in South-East Asia in Singapore in September 1945. Because General Terauchi was sick and unable to surrender in person, Mountbatten accepted the Japanese C-in-C's ceremonial sword at a later ceremony in Saigon.

Mountbatten returned to London to the plaudits of a nation euphoric at victory after wearisome years of war. He was created a Knight of the Order of the Garter, the six-hundred-year-old honour, and a viscount.

Youngest Supreme Commander of World War II, Admiral Lord Louis Mountbatten accepts a sword as a symbol of the Japanese surrender in Singapore in September 1945. (Broadlands Archives)

Mountbatten, now forty-six and 'promoted' to the substantive rank of Rear Admiral from Captain, was anxious to get back to sea; indeed, he was earmarked for command of the First Cruiser Squadron in the Mediterranean, but Prime Minister Clement Attlee had other plans for him.

Attlee summoned him to Downing Street where Mountbatten was stunned to be invited to succeed Lord Wavell as Viceroy of India, with the prime task of leading the nation to freedom from the British Crown. Mountbatten thus became the last Viceroy of India—and then the new Dominion's first Governor-General.

Soon after his return to England in 1948 Mountbatten took over the First Cruiser Squadron in the Mediterranean where the C-in-C was Admiral Sir Arthur Power who a few years earlier had commanded the East Indies Fleet under Mountbatten's command!

This brief appointment was brought to an end in 1949 when, after promotion to Vice Admiral, he soon returned to London where he remained for two years as Fourth Sea Lord responsible for Supplies and Transport.

As C-in-C Mountbatten once again returned to the Mediterranean—the scene of many royal naval appointments, from the derisive posting of Prince Edward Augustus and the more meritorious ones of Prince Alfred and of Prince Louis of Battenberg. But Mountbatten was to out-rank them all, for in May 1952 he assumed the role of NATO C-in-C, Allied Forces, Mediterranean, with authority over elements of the navies of France, the USA, Italy, Greece, Turkey and Britain, co-ordinating them all into an effective Allied fleet. It was yet another 'first' for Mountbatten.

Another 'double first', unique in the long history of the Royal Navy, occurred in 1955: one of the last acts of Winston Churchill, the then Prime Minister, was to appoint Mountbatten to the highest post in the navy—the First Sea Lord. In doing so, Churchill became the only man ever to have appointed a father and son to this key post; and equally uniquely Mountbatten and Prince Louis are the only father and son to have served as the professional head of the navy.

The navy over which Mountbatten presided bore little relationship to that which his father commanded nearly forty years before. Gone were the giant guns of the Jutland broadsides, gone too the ponderous majesty of the battleships and battle-cruisers, the awesome coal-burning battlesquadrons: power now rested in the aircraft of the fleet carriers, in the radar-controlled gun batteries, high-speed ships with close-range guided missiles, ships driven by gas turbined engines. Mountbatten inherited what was fundamentally a twofold task: firstly to trim down the navy to a slimmer but more athletic force; and secondly—and this appealed to him enormously—to modernize the navy still further by introducing nuclear propulsion, equipping the ships with devastating new weaponry and training crews in the new skills and technology of the emerging modern navy. It was an exciting and challenging period

" Only been Viceroy of India and First Sea Lord ! Why, he's 54 and still to get up to British Railways Chief, Prime Minister, and Director-General of Television."

This Cummings cartoon captures the Mountbatten image at this time.
(Daily Express)

of office which responded to Mount-batten's reforming and innovating zeal.

In July 1959 Mountbatten was appointed Chief of the Defence Staff and some years later he brought the three Service Ministers under a single unified Ministry of Defence, an unpopular reform in service circles, particularly in the navy where three hundred years of history in the form of the Board of Admiralty were cast aside as if, some said, in requital for his father's long past injustice.

In July 1965 the MOD job finished and after fifty-two years in the navy with the rank of Admiral of the Fleet Mountbatten virtually retired—Admirals of the Fleet do not, in fact, retire —his uniform seemingly swathed in gold lace and braided with colourful ribbons reflecting a nation's honours

Earl Mountbatten of Burma was killed by an assassin in Ireland in 1979. (Crown Copyright)

and decorations to a much respected royal sailor. Thus came to an end one of the Royal Navy's most brilliant and formidable careers.

The end of his life came in August 1979 through a cowardly assassin's bomb attack aboard his boat at Mullaghmore, County Sligo in the Irish Republic. Prince Alfred, Duke of Edinburgh, managed to survive a would-be assassin's bullet in the back; the cruel attack on Mountbatten's life by a remote radio-controlled bomb nearly a century later was tragically effective. Ironically he had survived the enemy's endeavours to kill him by sea and air in war, then fell to a sneak killer in peace. Mountbatten was for seventy-nine years a survivor, a warrior, a man of war yet paradoxically a man of peace; he died spectacularly and violently like so many of his relatives.

10

Prince Philip,
Duke of Edinburgh

THE BABY born on 10 June 1921 to the Prince and Princess Andrew of Greece on the island of Corfu was a third generation Mountbatten and some believe that had he stayed in the navy he would have had the potential to outstrip his illustrious uncle and his legendary maternal great-grandfather.

The island home of the future Duke of Edinburgh was the square Regency-style villa, Mon Repos, on a promontory providing views of the placid Ionian Sea. 'Impoverished' is a word applied to the family during their stay there and this is evidenced by the report that the property lacked electricity, gas and running hot water. The birth, it was feared, would be difficult, and by all accounts it took place on the dining room table.

The baby was the fifth child of the marriage: Prince Andrew was thirty-nine and at the time of the birth was fighting the Turks in Asia Minor: the thirty-six-year-old Princess Alice was Earl Mountbatten's eldest sister. She had been born with the handicap of deafness and learned to speak with difficulty in an unnaturally deep voice: by middle age she had become somewhat eccentric and a deeply religious person.

Prince Philip was born into the intricate tapestry of the Schleswig-Holstein-Sonnderburg-Glücksburg Royal House of Denmark, a family almost as complex as Battenberg's Hessian fabric. On his mother's side Philip was a great-great-grandson of Queen Victoria. Philip's grandfather was King George I of the Hellenes, who as the Danish naval cadet Prince William George in 1863, was selected to ascend the throne of Greece; Prince Alfred, it will be remembered, had been offered the crown but it was a reluctant young King George I (named after the Greek national saint) who landed at the

Piraeus and entered the chilling marble halls of the palace. Years of coping with political intrigues were rewarded in 1867 with a shy young Russian bride, the teenage Grand Duchess Olga. This union —the grandparents of Prince Philip—was the foundation of the royal house of Greece.

Queen Olga's first-born was given the name Constantine in memory of the last emperor of Byzantine Greece; there followed George, Nicholas, Andrew (Philip's father), Alexandra, Marie and Olga (who died in her year of birth). The marriages of these Princes and Princesses linked the Greek royal house with the Hohenzollerns and Bonapartes, with the Russian royal family and by Prince Andrew's marriage to Alice, with the Battenbergs. The bride's father, Admiral Prince Louis of Battenberg, instructed that the wedding ceremony be celebrated at Darmstadt's Old Palace and the guest list was impressive.

Philip's father narrowly escaped execution in the aftermath of the complex manœuvrings of war and politics in Asia Minor but his release was secured in exchange for the loss of his titles and banishment. He and his family, including the eighteen-month-old Philip, were evacuated from Greece to Rome in the light cruiser *Calypso* (Captain Gerald Talbot); Philip was provided with a padded orange crate to serve as a cot.

The family lived in Paris for some years where Philip went to a boarding school attended in the main by sons of wealthy American businessmen, until an invitation was received from George Mountbatten, Louis's older brother, the Second Marquess of Milford Haven, for Philip to stay with the Milford Havens at Lyndon Manor near Maidenhead. Philip, now aged nine, journeyed to England and for three years went to the Tabor School in Cheam with the Milford Haven's son, David.

George Milford Haven was to exert an influence upon the young Philip, acting as a foster father while Prince Andrew and Princess Alice, having got their four daughters off their hands by marriage to German princes, separated, Alice to devote herself wholeheartedly to the Nursing Order she joined and Andrew, in contrast, to live the life of a *boulevardier*. It was George, too, who directed Philip's attention to the navy in which George had served with credit in World War I, rather like Prince Alfred influenced young Battenberg all those years before at Heilingenberg. But Philip was to reveal later that neither George nor Earl Mountbatten had consciously influenced him to join the Royal Navy: he simply accepted the inevitable when the family made the decision for him.

The experience which most influenced Philip during his formative years of adolescence was the tough, monastic-like schooling under the tutorship of the German-Jewish founder, Dr Kurt Hahn. Prince Philip joined Hahn's school at Salem in the forested hills around Lake Constance, and later in Scotland where a new school was opened at Gordonstoun on the Moray Firth. It was a rigorous, harsh regimen but Philip responded well and during his last year was given the post of Guardian or Head Boy; as well as excelling in sailing he was captain of the cricket and hockey teams. Of Philip, Dr Hahn wrote: 'He is a born leader,' then added more presciently, 'but will need the exacting demands of a great service to do justice to himself.' However the great service he was to perform was not to be in the navy, but in an altogether different sphere—as consort to the Queen.

In the autumn of 1938 Philip's avuncular guardian and mentor George Milford Haven died of cancer and Philip came more directly under the influence of his other uncle, the dynamic Lord Mountbatten who now assumed responsibility for his young nephew. Notwithstanding Philip's later denials, the influence of these two eminent guardians and the young man's upbringing in a navy-dominated environment had left their imprints; both his grandfathers served at sea and both his father's and mother's brothers served in the navy. It gave Lord Mountbatten special satisfaction when, early in 1939, Philip passed his naval entry examination creditably enough, coming sixteenth out of thirty-four successful candidates, doing rather better in the oral examinations scoring 380 marks out of a possible 400.

He entered Dartmouth Naval College on 4 May 1939 and because of the onset of war he was only to spend eight months there during which time he applied himself zealously and competitively. He received the King's Dirk as the leading cadet of his term and the Eardley-Howard-Crockett award for the best all-round cadet of the year; with the latter went a book token which Philip exchanged for Captain Liddell Hart's strategic study, *The Defence of Britain*.

Prince Philip returns to the Royal Naval College, Dartmouth in 1972 to attend a celebration dinner held by his uncle, Earl Mountbatten of Burma. (Imperial War Museum)

The first day of the new year of destiny for Britain—1940—brought Philip's appointment as a midshipman to the old battle-ship HMS *Ramilles*, stationed at Colombo and engaged in escorting transports of Australian and New Zealand troops to the Mediter-ranean theatre. It was a safe but unsatisfying posting for a young midshipman. But the question of sending Philip to an active theatre raised some awkward doubts. He was still a foreign prince, albeit a neutral one, despite having applied for British citizenship: the con-sequences of Philip being captured or killed would be inconceiv-able and it was prudent to keep him out of harm's way; convoy work in the dull Indian Ocean seemed, to the diplomats, ideal.

Prince Philip recorded his midshipman's activities in his 'Journal for the use of Junior Officers Afloat'—the sturdily bound log which all midshipmen were compelled to keep during the whole of their sea-time—and 'produce at the examination in Seamanship for the rank of Lieutenant'. The objects of keeping the journal are to train midshipmen in the power of observation, the power of expression and the habit of orderliness.

Philip skilfully decorated his log with explanatory sketches and drawings and his narrative prowess improved as is illustrated by the entry describing the Festival of Pera-Hera at Kandy. Anyone who visited Kandy up-country in Ceylon to see the Temple of Tooth cannot help but be impressed by the visit let alone the spectacle of the Pera-Hera. Philip wrote:

> I counted 80 elephants in one of these processions all beautifully dressed with bright coloured sheets embroidered with silver and brass. All the old Kandy chiefs took part in these processions and they too were wonderful to look at. Four-cornered gold crowns on there [sic] heads then short beautifully embroidered jackets of purple velvet or silver and gold brocade. Then thirty yards of very fine white silk edged with gold, wound round their middles which made them look as if they had enormous stomachs. They had close fitting trousers on with pointed red leather shoes on their feet. Each of these chiefs was preceded by his dancers . . .

Philip faithfully recorded his visits to all those ports familiar to sailors who served in the Far East—Aden, Bombay, Trincomalee, Sydney, Mombasa and Durban: no British sailor who visited Durban could ever forget the welcoming friendship and hospitality generously dispensed by everyone ashore and much of it organized by the SAWAS (South African Women's Auxiliary Service). Philip was no exception: 'The grand unselfish hospitality with which we were welcomed by the people of Durban', he recorded, 'will live in our memories for years to come . . .'

In April Philip transferred from the elderly, ponderous *Ramilles* to the gunroom of the 9850-ton heavy cruiser *Kent* and within months he joined another 8-inch gun cruiser, the 9830-ton *Shropshire*. 'A few minutes after nine o'clock on Sunday October 1st 1940, I walked aboard His Majesty's Ship *Shropshire*, the third ship in eight months to receive this singular honour.' Philip was expressing his youthful resentment at yet another Indian Ocean appointment. He longed for a posting to the Mediterranean where the intervention of Italy into the war made this the most active theatre of war.

Within a month of his joining the *Shropshire* Italy took the incredibly ill-advised decision to invade Greece, an action which effectively lost Philip his neutral status. He immediately sought the intervention of none other than the First Sea Lord himself, Admiral Sir Dudley Pound, for a new posting. Whether as a result of this plea or not, Philip gained his wish.

In January 1941 he joined the 32,700-ton battleship *Valiant*, launched in World War I and twenty-seven years later still serving the nation. She was one of that splendid class of battleship—arguably the finest class of all time—the *Queen Elizabeth, Valiant, Warspite, Malaya* and *Barham*. Philip's hopes of action were soon realized. A few days after joining her, almost before he had had time to secure a berth for himself, *Valiant* took part in a bombardment of Bardia in support of General Wavell's advance into Cyrenaica.

Philip's action station was on the searchlight platform and from this vantage point he experienced for the first time the thunderous jolting of the ship's eight huge 15-inch guns and her fourteen 6-inch. Philip logged: 'We arrived off the coast . . . at dawn. In the dark the flashes of the guns could be seen a very long way out at sea. We went to action stations at 0730 and at 0810 the bombardment commenced . . . The whole operation was a very spectacular affair . . .' The guns of *Warspite, Valiant* and *Barham* brought about the surrender of the Italian garrison.

A few days later Philip experienced more action in one of those massive, organizational operations which became a feature of every convoy to beleaguered Malta. 'Excess' was the name given to the operation whose primary task was the replenishment of Malta.

Scores of vessels were engaged in a series of complicated moves over a period of several days in the face of attacks by Italian bombers, torpedo boats, a submarine and mines. On 10 January the C-in-C's Force was subjected to intensive air attacks in the course of which the *Illustrious* was hit by six heavy bombs. Philip described the scene:

At dawn action stations on Friday gun flashes were sighted on the starboard bow. We increased speed to investigate, and by the time we were within five miles it was almost daylight. *Bonaventure* signalled that *Southampton* and herself were engaging two enemy destroyers [actually the torpedo boats *Circe* and

Vega]. We could just see one of these . . . blowing up in a cloud of smoke and spray. The other escaped. Shortly after this the destroyer *Gallant* hit a mine and her bow was blown off, and floated slowly away on the swell . . . At noon two torpedo bombers attacked us, but a quick alteration of course foiled their attempt, and their fish passed down the port side. Shortly after this sixteen German dive bombers attacked the *Illustrious*. She was hit aft and amidships and fires broke out. Then the bombers concentrated on us and five bombs dropped fairly close . . .

Later in the month Philip flew by Sunderland aircraft to the Piraeus to make unexpected calls on his royal relations. 'They are an impoverished lot,' wrote Sir Henry (Chips) Channon unkindly in his diary.* Philip's mother greeted him joyously somehow coping with the dichotomy of her son serving in the Royal Navy and her sons-in-law as high-ranking German officers. Philip was entertained by the King, Crown Prince Paul, his wife Frederica and second cousin Alexandra. At a cocktail party at this time Chips Channon made a curious diary entry for 21 January 1941: '. . . Prince Philip of Greece was there. He is extraordinarily handsome . . . He is to be our Prince Consort, and that is why he is serving in our Navy. He is charming, but I deplore such a marriage: he and Princess Elizabeth are too inter-related.' It was a remarkable entry. There could not possibly have been even an understanding at that time of Philip marrying Princess Elizabeth yet Channon's diary is unequivocal.†

In Admiral Cunningham the navy had one of the greatest sailors since Nelson and Philip was privileged to have served under him in one of the most dramatic phases of the Battle of Cape Matapan, the first main fleet action in which carrier-borne aircraft played an indispensable role in defence, search and attack. It was the first time that radar-equipped ships detected and tracked down unsuspecting enemy ships and brought them to battle. Cunningham's victory at

---

* *Chips: The Diaries of Sir Henry Channon*, ed. Robert Rhodes James, Weidenfeld & Nicholson, 1967.
† A later entry in February 1944 showed less certainty: 'I do believe that a marriage may well be arranged one day between Princess Elizabeth and Prince Philip of Greece.'

sea was timely and significant for it established naval supremacy over a powerful Italian fleet and a strengthening Luftwaffe presence in the eastern basin of the Mediterranean.

The battle was fought on 28 and 29 March 1941 in the seas to the south and west of Crete with the main action taking place about 100 miles off Cape Matapan in Greece, which gave its name to the battle.

Cunningham led his battle fleet from Alexandria: the carrier *Formidable* had replaced the damaged *Illustrious* and she was accompanied by *Warspite*, *Valiant* and *Barham* with nine escorting destroyers. The fleet made a rendezvous with four cruisers under the command of Vice Admiral Pridham-Whippell.

The combined British forces located and pursued Admiral Angelo Iachino in his fine battleship, the 41,167-tons *Vittorio Veneto*, five accompanying heavy cruisers and several destroyers. A strike by *Formidable*'s aircraft resulted in one torpedo hit on the flagship. The *Vittorio Veneto*'s speed was reduced to 19 knots but she continued on her course. A second air strike by torpedo bombers launched after sunset hit and disabled the 11,500-ton heavy cruiser *Pola* (Captain M. de Pisa). She was left behind to cope as well as she could.

After a while Iachino ordered the other two heavy cruisers of the First Cruiser Squadron, the *Zara* (Captain L. Cossi) and *Fiume* (Captain G. Giorgis)—together with destroyers—to turn back to take the *Pola* in tow.

Presently the British battleships' radar established contact with the crippled cruiser and crews went to action station. The returning Italian cruisers and the 9th Destroyer Flotilla were sighted as silhouettes steaming across the bows of the battle fleet quite unaware of the presence of their enemy. The British ships were steaming in line ahead: *Warspite*, *Valiant*, *Formidable*, *Barham*. The Italian ships were led by the destroyer *Alfieri* followed by the cruisers *Zara*, *Fiume* and the destroyers *Gioberti*, *Carducci* and *Oriani*.

At this time there was a formidable array of guns trained on the Italian ships: twenty-four 15-inch, twenty 6-inch and twenty 4.5-inch. By contrast the guns of the enemy were trained fore and aft; the enemy was completely oblivious of the terror to befall them.

The destroyer *Greyhound* exposed searchlights quickly followed by those of *Valiant*. Simultaneously *Warspite* and *Valiant* opened fire on the *Fiume* at ranges of 2900 and 4000 yards. In three minutes of violent action the destroyer *Alfieri* had been blasted to destruction by two heavy salvoes from *Barham*. The *Zara*, second in line, was shot to pieces by four broadsides from *Warspite*, five from *Valiant* and five from *Barham*. The *Fiume*, third in line, had been hit by two broadsides from *Warspite* and one from *Valiant*. Later, the *Pola* was located and sunk by the 14th Destroyer Flotilla, and the *Havock* torpedoed and sank the *Carducci*.

Prince Philip watched from the vantage point on the *Valiant*'s searchlight platform; he recorded in his journal:

HMS Valiant *firing a broadside. Prince Philip served aboard her during the aerial bombardment of Crete and the Battle of Cape Matapan in 1941. (Imperial War Museum)*

I switched on our midship light which picked out the enemy cruiser and lit her up as if it were broad daylight. She was only seen complete in the light for a few seconds as the flagship had already opened fire, and as her first broadside landed and she was blotted out from just abaft the bridge to right astern. We fired our first broadside about 7 seconds after the flagship . . . the broadside only consisted of A and B turrets as the after turret would not bear. By now all the secondary armament of both ships had opened fire and the noise was considerable. The Captain and the Gunnery Officer now began shouting from the bridge for the searchlights to train left. The idea that there might have been another ship, with the one we were firing at never entered my head, so it was some few moments before I was persuaded to relinquish the blazing target and search for another one I had no reason to believe was there. However, training to the left, the light picked up another cruiser, ahead of the first one by three or four cables. As the enemy was so close the light did not illuminate the whole ship but only about three quarters of it, so I trained left over the whole ship until the bridge structure was in the centre of the beam. The effect was rather like flashing a strong torch on a small model about 5 yards away . . . She was illuminated in an undamaged condition for the period of about 5 seconds when our second broadside left the ship, and almost at once she was blotted out from stem to stern . . . Four more broadsides were fired at the enemy . . . When the enemy had completely vanished in clouds of smoke and steam we ceased firing and switched the light off.

For his actions that night Philip's name figured among the many who were mentioned in despatches.

A few weeks after the Battle of Cape Matapan another battle dominated the naval scene in the eastern basin of the Mediterranean: it was the protracted battle for the island of Crete with its long drawn-out fierce ordeals for the navy. Prince Philip's journal entry for the third day of the battle—22 May—put it succinctly:

Next day things began to get worse. *Juno* [destroyer] was sunk. *Naiad* and *Carlisle* [cruisers] were hit. A signal came asking for assistance, so we turned and steamed at 20 knots . . . As we came in sight of the straits we saw *Naiad* and *Carlisle* being attacked by bombers. We went right in to within 10 miles of Crete and then the bombing started in earnest. Stukas came over but avoided the big ships and went for the crippled cruisers and destroyer screens. *Greyhound* was hit right aft by a large bomb, her stern blew up and she sank about twenty minutes later. *Gloucester* and *Fiji* [cruisers] were sent in to help . . . Three Me 109s attacked *Warspite* as dive bombers and she was hit just where her starboard forrard mounting was . . . When we had got about 15 miles from the land 16 Stukas came out and attacked two cruisers. *Gloucester* was badly hit and sank some hours later . . . We were bombed from a high level by a large number of small bombs in sticks of 12 or more. One Dornier came straight for us from the port beam and dropped 12 bombs when he was almost overhead. We turned to port and ceased firing, when suddenly the bombs came whistling down, landing very close all down the port side . . . It was only some time later that I discovered we had been hit twice on the quarterdeck. One bomb exploded just abaft the quarterdeck screen on the port side . . . the other landed within twenty feet of it, just inboard of the port rails, blowing a hole into the wardroom laundry . . . There were only four casualties.

The journal continued with the dismal story: '*Calcutta* [cruiser] was sunk. *Nubian* [destroyer] had her stern blown off . . . *Orion* was hit by two bombs, one of them completely wrecked A turret, the other went in through the bridge, down five decks and exploded making an enormous hole and killing 140 sailors and 200 soldiers being evacuated.'* For almost a week this went on, day after day ships coming in to Alexandria packed with troops, destroyers showing not-under-control balls, cruisers peppered with shrapnel holes from near misses.

On 23 May more losses were suffered when Lord Mountbatten's

---

* Prince Philip's contemporary record errs in detail but the picture of war at sea that he paints is graphic. The cruiser *Orion* suffered 107 sailors lost and 155 soldiers killed. More than 300 men were wounded. *Gloucester* sank with the loss of 725 lives: *Fiji* with 271 missing.

5th Destroyer Flotilla was dive-bombed and the *Kelly* and *Kashmir* were sunk. HMS *Kipling* brought the exhausted survivors—including Mountbatten—to the sanctuary of Alexandria amid cheers from every ship in harbour. Prince Philip was one of the first to greet his bedraggled uncle as Mountbatten came ashore.

In June Philip returned home with other midshipmen for their sub-lieutenant courses, travelling aboard the *Duchess of Atholl*, embarking at Port Said for the Cape—a long way home but non-essential traffic was not routed through the violent Mediterranean.

At Cape Town Philip was entertained royally by his Greek relations; the exiled George II and his family were comfortably quartered in Groote Schuur, the home of General Smuts near Cape Town.

The journey home proved longer than expected. At Cape Town Philip's party of midshipmen transferred to another ship heading for Halifax, Nova Scotia to join a UK-bound convoy. At Puerto Rico the Chinese stokers, fearing the prospects of an Atlantic crossing deserted en masse and Philip and other naval personnel taking passage buckled to and laboured hard wielding shovels in the scorching heat of the boiler room.

In the courses that Prince Philip now took at Portsmouth and Greenwich he performed magisterially, obtaining four Firsts and a Second in his examinations, earning himself nine months seniority out of a possible ten. On 1 February 1942 he put up his first stripe and took up his appointment in the old 1918 flotilla leader *Wallace* of 1480 tons and mounting four 4-inch guns. She was a far cry from *Valiant* and lacked the modernity and élan of a *Kelly*.

The *Wallace* was one of many warships engaged on the tedious coastal convoy work between Rosyth and Sheerness—known as E-boat Alley—which challenged the escorts not only with E-boats but with acoustic, magnetic and contact mines, with air attacks by bombers and strafing by fighters. For eighteen months Philip persevered with the tedium and hazards of the east coast work, compensated by promotion to Lieutenant in July and then in October he was made First Lieutenant. Twenty-one was young to be First Lieutenant of a destroyer and Philip brought the zest of youth to this executive officer's job and aimed to make *Wallace* the crack ship. But there was tough competition for this role from a young

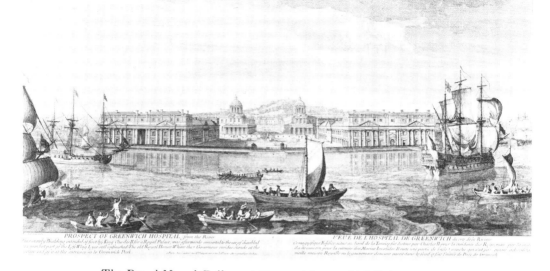

The Royal Naval College at Greenwich, to which Prince Philip returned in 1941 after a heavy bout of naval action. The beautiful Wren building was originally designed as a hospital for wounded seamen. It became a college of higher education for officers in 1873. (National Maritime Museum)

Australian First Lieutenant, Michael Parker aboard the *Lauderdale*, from which rivalry sprang a friendship which was to last for many years.

In mid-1943 the increasing Allied activity in the Mediterranean called for naval reinforcements and in July the *Wallace* sailed from Scapa to give support to the invasion of Sicily. Towards the end of the year she sailed home for a refit. Philip undertook further courses at Greenwich and was ashore for the next eight months.

For much of this time he stayed at Mountbatten's home in Chester Street in Belgravia. Mountbatten was now in South-East Asia while Lady Edwina was still in London, busily engaged in her duties for the Red Cross and St John's Ambulance Services. Christmas of that year was spent as a guest of the royal family at Windsor Castle and Philip related his experiences of the Sicily landings to King George VI who always retained a deep interest in all matters naval.

In the new year of 1944 Philip was appointed First Lieutenant of the new destroyer *Whelp* still building in Hebburn Yard on the

Tyne. She displaced 1710 tons and was armed with four 4.7-inch guns and had a speed in excess of 36 knots.

Now that the Normandy landings had succeeded and the battle of northern Europe was raging, the focus of naval attention was centred on the Far East and it was to Mountbatten's South-East Asia Command that the newly formed 27th Destroyer Flotilla, of which the *Whelp* was a unit, was despatched. Admiral Sir James Somerville was the C-in-C of the British East Indies Fleet and the 27th Destroyer Flotilla took part in fleet exercises and operations off Burma, the Andamans and Sumatra where the Royal Navy was increasingly displaying its dominance. As the tide of war flowed out of the Indian Ocean into the Pacific the 27th Flotilla sailed east to join Admiral Sir Bruce Fraser's British Pacific Fleet in the inexorable steamrolling defeat of the Japanese.

When the final surrender came—after the atomic bombs at Nagasaki and Hiroshima—the *Whelp* was one of the British ships which attended the assembly for the signing of the Instrument of Surrender aboard Admiral Halsey's flagship, the USS *Missouri* in Tokyo Bay on 2 September 1945. Ten days later Mountbatten accepted the sword of surrender at Singapore.

Whelp returned to Portsmouth in 1946 and Prince Philip decommissioned her after which he was appointed to the training establishment HMS *Glendower* at Pwllheli: two months later he took up a similar post at Corsham in Wiltshire, a cluster of cheerless Nissen huts named HMS *Port Arthur*, where Philip instructed petty officers and lectured them on strategy and naval affairs.

Early in 1947 he was naturalized as a British subject, his name appearing in the *London Gazette* along with hundreds of aliens and refugees from Europe, and he took as his surname, his uncle's, Mountbatten. Later that year he married HRH the Princess Elizabeth, the future Queen Elizabeth II. On the day before the wedding Philip Mountbatten was created Duke of Edinburgh, taking the title of an earlier royal sailor, Baron Greenwich and Earl of Merioneth and had bestowed on him the dignity of Royal Highness.

Marriage and his royal duties did not end Philip's naval career: he was appointed to the Operations Division of the Admiralty where he remained for a few months before, in March 1948, he progressed to a long and absorbing Staff Course at Greenwich

Naval College. A sea appointment came along in October 1949 and Philip, now the father of a baby son, joined the 1710 ton destroyer *Chequers* in Malta as First Lieutenant. On arrival in Malta Philip was met by his uncle, Mountbatten, then commanding the First Cruiser Squadron. Princess Elizabeth soon joined her husband and they stayed with the Mountbattens at the Villa Guardamangia near Pieta. When Mountbatten returned home to be Fourth Sea Lord the young couple took over the house. It was a pleasant, easy-going period with Philip able to indulge in his love of polo playing and the Princess leading a life as free from protocol as was possible. Philip coped with the curious need to respond to being called 'Number One' aboard the *Chequers* and calling his commanding officer 'Sir' yet ashore Lieutenant the Duke of Edinburgh took precedence over his C-in-C.

In July 1950 Philip earned his half stripe to become Lieutenant-Commander and in September he received the coveted appointment to HMS *Magpie* in command. In his command examinations Philip had failed, in fact, in Torpedo and ASDIC, subjects which he had to sit again.

Philip displayed the Mountbatten determination to win when in command; determined that his frigate should be Cock of the Fleet. It was a tough assignment for the crew, and they were worked hard: endeavour was rewarded and the *Magpie*'s boat's crew won six out of ten events in the annual regatta with Philip himself rowing stroke in one of the events.

In addition to the normal duties of a frigate's commanding officer Philip undertook a number of official and semi-official visits to kings and presidents; he performed other official duties in Gibraltar, in Algeria and Cyprus and in the early summer of 1950 he undertook a specially pleasurable visit to Athens. As the *Magpie* lacked the appropriate cabin accommodation to convey Princess Elizabeth from Malta to Greece the C-in-C made available HMS *Surprise*, enabling the Princess—soon to be Queen Elizabeth and Lord High Admiral—to travel in comfort. They were entertained ashore by Philip's cousins, King Paul and Queen Frederica, enjoying the informality of picnic and beach parties.

A year later in 1951 the writing was already on the wall and Philip's naval days were numbered. The King was a sick man and

*HRH Prince Philip, Duke of Edinburgh, as Admiral of the Fleet.
(Imperial War Museum)*

Princess Elizabeth, heir presumptive, was needed at home to share the burden of official duties and Philip was needed by her side. In July 1951 he was granted indefinite leave, left Malta and the *Magpie*—his first and last command. He had served a little over twelve years in the navy, the last year of which he declared had been the happiest of his naval life.

Sixteen months after the accession of Elizabeth to the throne a Supplement to the *London Gazette* made the announcement 'Her Majesty the Queen has been graciously pleased to approve the following promotion: Commander His Royal Highness the Duke of Edinburgh KG, KT, Royal Navy, to be Admiral of the Fleet.'

Huge question marks overshadow the back-cloth to Philip's naval career. Unquestionably able as a naval officer, with great promotional prospects before him—even at the age of thirty-two as a Commander he was clearly marked out as a candidate of potential flag rank—and undeniably developing great administrative skills and possessing those indefinable qualities of leadership, Philip stood on the threshold of achieving something approaching greatness . . . The long arduous years of devotion to the demanding, sometimes restrictive and often tiresome duties of Prince Consort have confirmed many of the qualities seen in him as a serving naval officer. But the questions which remain unanswered are those relating to what-might-have-been. Would he *really* have made flag rank? Or, having achieved it, would he have become a C-in-C, let alone First Sea Lord? Would he have begun to match some of the great achievements of Uncle Dickie, with whom he must inevitably be compared? Or does Mountbatten stand somehow supreme even in the ranks of royal admirals? Was Mountbatten served well by the circumstances of war, while the later years of Philip's career would have been devoted to the cause of peace rather than the execution of war. Would Philip have out-shone his illustrious Battenberg ancestor, Prince Louis, First Sea Lord under Churchill's tenancy of the Admiralty in World War I? The questions seem endless: the speculation and hypothesising lead nowhere. Suffice it to say that the mere debating of the subject presupposes a likelihood of Philip attaining something at least equal to the greatness of his naval forebears.

11

Prince Charles, Prince of Wales

IT WAS a wintry February day in the austere postwar year of 1952 when Queen Elizabeth succeeded to the throne and the three-year-old Prince Charles became the Heir Apparent. His future career would be prescribed by protocol: gone would be any choice of a permanent professional career in the navy. Traditionally and historically the heir to the throne has been directed towards a military career. If protocol was to be observed then Charles would be expected to soldier his way to the throne. But in the excitingly unpredictable style of his father and great-uncle he served for a period in the Royal Air Force and the Royal Navy—giving the army a wide berth.

Charles was born in Buckingham Palace on 14 November 1948. His ancestry was incredibly cosmopolitan: Scandinavia, Anjou, Scotland, Greece, Normandy, Wales, Germany, Holland, Russia, all these provided threads in the tapestry of Charles's ancestry: generations upon generations of kings, dukes, counts and princes link families of royal lineage in the genealogical table of his forebears: he is thirty-ninth in descent from the great King who helped found a navy, and began this naval story—King Alfred.

In 1971 the twenty-three-year-old Prince Charles, graduate of Trinity College, Cambridge, pilot in the RAF, entered the Royal Navy with the rank of Sub-Lieutenant for a graduate officer course. He reported for duty at the Royal Naval College, Dartmouth where his father and grandfather had started on their careers as cadets. Prince Philip commented at the time: 'The Royal Navy will provide the best training for the Prince of Wales. It has several advantages as a training ground . . . Aboard ship you learn to live with people, this is the important thing.'

197

The Dartmouth course was an intensive six weeks of instruction and study in seamanship, navigation, marine and electrical engineering and duties of a divisional officer. Practical work in ship handling, seamanship and coastal navigation were undertaken in a 360-ton minesweeper, the *Walkerton*, which was attached to the college. Intensive though it may have been, the short course contrasted starkly with the years' long training of Dartmouth cadets of old whose whole life became navy-influenced from the age of thirteen or so, a system which produced officers of the highest calibre who distinguished not only themselves in World War II but the ships in which they served, the service to which they had dedicated themselves and the college which had influenced them so profoundly in their early, formative years.

Prince Charles excelled in the passing-out examinations, coming top in both navigation and seamanship, perhaps the two most important subjects for an executive officer. Great-uncle Lord Mountbatten attended the passing out parade with pride in the young Prince's achievements.

Charles put theory to practical use aboard the 5600-ton guided missile destroyer HMS *Norfolk* (Captain J. W. D. Cook) which he joined in November 1971 and served aboard her for a little over eight months while working for his watch-keeping certificate. He then joined the shore establishment of HMS *Dryad* for further courses and training before joining the submarine shore base at Gosport—HMS *Dolphin*—where he underwent the dangerous submarine escape drill in a hundred-feet tank of water, permission for which was required from the Queen and the Prime Minister.

A succession of appointments over the next few years took Charles to the coastal minesweeper *Glasserton*, the Leander-class frigate *Minerva* in the Caribbean, aboard which he received his promotion to Lieutenant; the small hydrographic vessel *Fox*, the frigate *Jupiter*, alongside in Singapore and the commando carrier *Hermes* as a naval helicopter pilot in which he visited Canada and the USA.

Early in 1976 Charles completed an advanced course at the Royal Naval College, Greenwich, before receiving the treasured appointment to HMS *Bronington*—'in command'. This unpretentious mine-hunter of 360 tons was a wooden-hulled vessel, reverting in

HRH Prince Charles, Prince of Wales, as a lieutenant in 1973.
(Imperial War Museum)

a sense to the vessels of a hundred years before; one of the smallest, least prestigious ships in the modern navy, she was, nevertheless,

Charles's command and he enjoyed the man management entailed, but not the unmerciful rolling at sea of which the ship was capable.

It was flying which Charles found more satisfying and after a helicopter flying course in 1974 he told an interviewer: 'I adore flying and I personally can't think of a better combination than naval flying.' At twenty-six the young prince had matured considerably and was fast becoming a man for all seasons, a jack of all trades . . . and possibly master of none?

Pride in command was well understood by Charles's father who elected to visit his son's mine-hunter and it was at Rosyth that Lieutenant HRH the Prince of Wales welcomed aboard Admiral of the Fleet HRH the Duke of Edinburgh who acknowledged the piping side party and proceeded to inspect the ship.

It was December 1976 when Prince Charles retired from active service of five years in the Royal Navy having maintained the honourable family tradition of naval service performed by his father, grandfather, great-grandfather, great-uncle and many others before that. Charles's younger brother, Prince Andrew, the Queen's second son, will undoubtedly be permitted to pursue his chosen naval career without let or hindrance; he could well achieve the rank of his predecessor, Prince Alfred, Duke of Edinburgh, and reach flag rank by personal endeavour. It will be particularly interesting to follow the career of this young naval Prince who has the potential to achieve great things in the Royal Navy: it is an exciting prospect. He has much family naval tradition from which to draw strength, not least of which is the guidance, advice and example of his father who might have achieved greatness in the navy and the high example of his great-uncle, who did.

INDEX